MW00807032

# Daily Devotions and Random Thoughts for You or Someone You Know

LARRY HILL

ISBN 978-1-0980-8152-2 (paperback)
ISBN 978-1-0980-8153-9 (digital)

Copyright © 2021 by Larry Hill

All rights reserved. No part of this publication may be reproduced, distributed, or transmitted in any form or by any means, including photocopying, recording, or other electronic or mechanical methods without the prior written permission of the publisher. For permission requests, solicit the publisher via the address below.

Christian Faith Publishing, Inc.
832 Park Avenue
Meadville, PA 16335
www.christianfaithpublishing.com

Printed in the United States of America

# Daily Devotions

———◆◆◆———

Good morning! Read Psalm 90:4 and Isaiah 49:16, then 2 Peter 3:8–9. We all have a past, live in the present, and wonder what the future holds. We all live within the boundaries of time. Only God lives outside of time. Time was created by God, and God is not governed by His creation but governs His creation. With God, the future *is* the present! God holds His children in the palm of His hand to bring their future into the present through hope, faith, and trust. God bless and much love.

# Daily Devotions

———◇◆◇———

Good morning! Read Luke 9:23–26 and Galatians 2:20. For any seed to bear any fruit, the seed must die first. This process is also true for anyone who comes to Christ. We must die to ourselves and be "born again" in the spirit! To crucify ourselves so Christ may live in us. It's then we desire to "take up the cross of Christ" and make it a daily practice in our lives. To witness for Christ as we witness to others that Christ lives in us! Being committed to Christ and no longer committed to who we once were! God bless and much love.

# Daily Devotions

———◈◈◈———

Good morning! Read Psalm 103:1–5. There's an old saying, "Never forget where you came from!" Yet many *do* forget! Especially the things God has done for them in their life. The healing power of God when they've been sick. The mercy God has shown in the forgiveness of sins. The patience and grace of God when we've taken credit, although it is God that makes all things possible. The very truth that we have life itself is of God. Let's *not* forget but give God thanks daily. Rejoice in His *love* for us! God bless and much love.

# Daily Devotions

———◇◇◇◇◇———

Good morning! Read 2 Corinthians 6:14–18. Water and oil cannot be mixed, and neither should a believer in Christ be mixed among the unbelievers. Their associations can be toxic in your development and growth in Christ! Unfortunately, there are many who are toxic to themselves! Knowing what to do but not doing it and knowing what to avoid but not avoiding it! Often becoming their own worst enemy! It's through Christ that you separate yourself from what's toxic in you to develop and grow in Him! God bless and much love.

# Daily Devotions

———◇◇◇◇◇———

Good morning! Read Romans 5:3–5 and James 1:2–4. Things grow in stages. The beginning leads to the middle, and the middle can determine the end. The end is determined by the overall growth! Our faith, hope, and trust in God are determined by the obstacles we overcome in our pursuit of God. The trying of our faith develops our patience, and through our patience, we gain experience. The experience we experience in God gives us hope to keep growing in Christ! A hope we are not ashamed to have in God! God bless and much love.

# Daily Devotions

———◇◆◇———

Good morning! Read Numbers 23:19 and Psalm 12:6, then Proverbs 30:5. Is there any word truer than God's Word? Is there any word that has greater power than the Word of God? Can anyone keep a promise the way God keeps His? Is there any god like our God? Can anyone deliver and save the way God does? His love and peace are there for the taking to all who submit themselves unto Him. His love abounds to all who call upon His name. God bless and much love.

# Daily Devotions

---

Good morning! Read James 2:19 and 1 Peter 5:6–11. Every child of God that lives in the power of God is an enemy and threat to the devil. The devil doesn't waste time attacking others like he does the children of God. The devil knows he's been defeated by the blood of Christ at the cross and is attempting to take as many as he can down with him. Therefore, we must be sober minded in our thinking. Not letting our guard down as to give the devil an opportunity to influence our life in any way. Not ceasing from prayer but staying "prayed up!" God bless and much love.

# Daily Devotions

———◇◇◇◇◇———

Good morning! Read John 20:29 and 2 Corinthians 4:18, then Hebrews 11:1. For many, seeing is believing! There must be tangible proof of something before they even consider believing! With God, just the opposite is true. It's our hope by way of faith that we believe that God calls into being the things that are not. Understanding it is having full confidence in our faith that moves God to bring into being what may be impossible for the nonbeliever to see and understand! But we see because we do understand! God bless and much love.

# Daily Devotions

———◈◈◈◈◈———

Good morning! Read Matthew 25:31–46. The followers of Christ are to reflect the Light of Christ to all we see. To reflect the Light of Christ, we must have the compassion of Christ for others. To do the things that are Christlike in love and respect and thoughtfulness to those in need. To be a helping hand and a comfort to those who need comforting. By doing the things and living our life unto Christ, we prove we are the disciples of Christ and children of the most high God! God bless and much love.

# Daily Devotions

———◇≫≪≫◇———

G ood morning! Read Isaiah 26:3–4. You may not be the kind of person that everyone wants, but if you are in Christ Jesus, you are the kind of person everyone needs! To see and experience the calmness that is found by living within the ring of peace in God. It's by going outside of the ring of peace that we experience turmoil, stress, anxiety, worry, and fear in our life. But living and abiding in God's ring of peace, we are safe and enjoy the pleasures of God's love! Trust God and receive His peace! God bless and much love.

# Daily Devotions

---✦◈◈◈◈◈✦---

G ood morning! Read 2 Chronicles 15:2 and Revelation 3:20–22. God is every-where but will not go where He's not wanted. God has given us an invitation to live and abide in Him, but we must invite God to abide and live in us. God is with us as long as we are with Him. If we forsake Him, God will forsake us. God is calling and knocking at the door of our heart. It's up to us to answer the call and open the door of our heart. No one ever wants to miss an opportunity for something good. No opportunity is better than having God in your life. God bless and much love.

# Daily Devotions

---

Good morning! Read Isaiah 40:28–31 and 1 Corinthians 13:3–7, then Ephesians 4:26–32. How do you measure strength in the character of someone? Controlling your emotions in times of anger shows strength. Not doing so exposes weakness. To forgive shows strength. To be unforgiving does not. To love unconditionally takes strength. The weak lack this understanding. But the greatest strength comes from God when we wait on Him. God bless and much love.

# Daily Devotions

---

Good morning! Read 1 Samuel 17:45–50 and Isaiah 54:17. Every one of us represent something. Whether it's the company we work for or the school we attend or our family or who we are, there is an image we present. When we live to represent God, it's His name and image that shines in our lives. To deliver us out of the hands of those who oppress us and to protect us in His hands! The story of David and Goliath is an example of what God can do for all who live to represent Him. God bless and much love.

# Daily Devotions

———◆◇◆◇◆———

Good morning! Read Ezekiel 36:24–29 and 37:5, then 2 Corinthians 5:17. There are many who are tired and unsatisfied with the life they're living. Looking and hoping for a change and a fresh start in life. The only one who can give you the change and fresh start that will last that is desired is the change and fresh start given by God! God can give you the heart and mind to begin a new life in Him that is more than satisfying beyond your imagination! But you must trust Him to do so! God bless and much love.

# Daily Devotions

———◈◈◈◈◈———

Good morning! Read Job 23:12 and Psalm 119:11. We all have priorities in life. But what's important or a priority to you may be different from someone else's priority of importance. However, if you are in Christ, your most important priority is your relationship with God! You improve and grow in your relationship with God through knowing and understanding His Word! God's Word is spiritual food for the growing spirit within you. To keep you in the ways and will of God! God bless and much love.

# Daily Devotions

———◇✕✕✕✕◇———

Good morning! Read 2 Chronicles 15 verses 2 and 7, then 16:9 and Galatians 6:9. We cannot see the blowing of the wind, but we feel it. We cannot tell where it's coming from or where it's going. The Spirit of God is also constantly moving. However, the Spirit of God is moving with a purpose in searching the hearts of those in search of God and allowing God to perfect their life in Christ! God is with you to strengthen you in your well doing. His blessings will bless you in its due seasons! God bless and much love.

# Daily Devotions

———◇◈◇———

Good morning! Read Psalm 61 and 46:10, then Isaiah 26:3–4. Many live very busy and complicated lives. Never finding time or having very little time to acknowledge God and give God thanks. This is all brought about by the evil one to keep our mind off God. I encourage you to take the time and acknowledge God. Give Him your time because He gives us all His time. God honors those who honor Him (1 Samuel 2:30). God bless and much love.

# Daily Devotions

---

G ood morning! Read Isaiah 42:10–13 and 43:2, then 54:17. There are times in life when everything you do seems to be an uphill battle. When one problem is solved another is on the horizon. It's extremely important that we don't lose heart but keep looking to God. We may face discouragement at times, but it's the strength of God that strengthens us. God will never leave us. When you feel alone, know that you're not alone. He is always there to save those who are His. God is there to help. Though some may abandon God, God will never abandon us. God bless and much love.

# Daily Devotions

———◇◆◇———

Good morning! Read Judges 6:12–16.
It's often said and much believed that "strength is in numbers" and "more is better." But when God is on our side, the numbers of the opposition does not matter! God can cause the few to triumph over the many and enable what is less to be blessed over what is more. To make what seems impossible possible! But we must look to God! Knowing and believing God has the power to do so! It's His strength and not ours that we are able to overcome! God bless and much love.

# Daily Devotions

———⟨◇⟩———

Good morning! Read Matthew 13:54–58 and Galatians 2:20. Living a new life in Christ can be difficult to understand for those who have known you most or all your life. They see you as you were and not as who you are now! They understand your old natural life but have difficulty comprehending and understanding your new spiritual walk in Christ Jesus! That you have laid down your old natural life to live a new spiritual life! However, how you live is the best example of who you've become in Christ! God bless and much love.

# Daily Devotions

---

Good morning! Read Psalm 37:23–24 and 37 and 1 Corinthians 10:1–4. God is delighted in those who are good and guides their steps. God upholds them and leads them into associations with others who are good and righteous before God. Having a common mindset of following the perfect man who is Christ Jesus! Being sustained and fed by the Word of God and drinking from that spiritual rock and that rock is Christ! Following the example *of* Christ Jesus to be an example *for* Christ Jesus! God bless and much love.

# Daily Devotions

---

Good morning! Read Romans 12:9–21. Often we are gravitated to certain things. For some, it is certain foods or drinks. For others, it may be certain places, people, or things. To evildoers, it's to do more evil, and to the righteous, it's to be more righteous. The righteous turn away from the evil and strive to be kindly affectioned to others. Being forgiving with love and rejoicing in hope of the righteousness of God. Not being overcome with evil but overcoming evil with the righteousness of that which is good! God bless and much love.

# Daily Devotions

---

Good morning! Read Psalm 39:3–5 and John 5:24, then Revelation 22:12–13. There are many insects whose lifespan is less than a day. Just a day compared to the years that we live. Yet the years that we live are less than a moment in time or the blink of an eye compared to the eternal infinite life of God. It's a blessing to live at all, and our life is even more blessed when we receive the eternal blessing of eternal life. Received by believing in Jesus Christ our Lord. God bless and much love.

# Daily Devotions

―――――◈◈◈◈◈◈◈◈―――――

Good morning! Read Luke 13:10–16. All of us have been bound by some sort of bondage, whether it's our health, our finances, relationships with our parents, children, or significant other. Quite often it can last for years. Much of this is the result of Satan at work in our lives to keep us from where God would have us to be. Jesus attributed the woman bound with an infirmity for eighteen years as a result of the workings of Satan. Yet He healed her by His Word. One Word from God can heal whatever has us bound also. God bless and much love.

# Daily Devotions

———◈◈◈———

Good morning! Read Ezekiel 3:17–21 and James 5:1920. When we see someone doing something that could be harmful, it is our responsibility to give them warning of the possible outcome if they continue what they're doing. God has made His children watchmen to the world to give the wrongdoers warning of their sinful ways. When we don't, there is a feeling of guilt. But when we do, we are free from the guilt of not doing so. We also save a soul from death and hide a multitude of our own sins! God bless and much love.

# Daily Devotions

———◆———

Good morning! Read Psalm 34:3–8. There are times we have questions and search for the answers only to find those answers bring about more questions. To satisfy the unknown, it's always wise to go to the highest source, and that source is God! It's God that will guide you to the answers to deliver you from the fears of the unknown. All are blessed that put their trust in Him. It's the angels of God that surround us, and it's the Spirit of God that guides us to the answers to the questions that we seek! God bless and much love.

# Daily Devotions

———◇◇◇◇◇———

G ood morning! Read Psalm 34:3–8. There are times we have questions and search for the answers only to find those answers bring about more questions. To satisfy the unknown, it's always wise to go to the highest source and that source is God! It's God that will guide you to the answers to deliver you from the fears of the unknown. All are blessed that put their trust in Him. It's the angels of God that surround us and it's the Spirit of God that guides us to the answers to the questions that we seek! God bless and much love.

# Daily Devotions

---

Good morning! Read Psalm 90:12 and 95:7–11, then 2 Corinthians 6:2. There are many who want to enjoy life in their own way and on their own terms before they come to God. Feeling they're not ready and need more time. Not considering there are many cemeteries filled with many who felt they weren't ready and needed more time! God has called and given the invitation of salvation! Be receptive to the calling of God to you! Today is the day of salvation! Tomorrow may be too late! God bless and much love.

# Daily Devotions

———◈◈◈———

G ood morning! Read Proverbs 3:5–6. A strong relationship with someone takes time to build. You must be willing to invest the time and effort to build the necessary trust and learn as much as you can about them. To be comfortable with their likes and dislikes and do all you can to gain their trust and confidence in you. A strong relationship with God takes the same type of effort! You must invest your time to learn to trust God! To learn His likes and dislikes and to grow your faith as your relationship with God grows! God bless and much love.

# Daily Devotions

---

Good morning! Read Judges 6:12–16 and 1 Corinthians 1:26–31. God has shown His concerns about those who are oppressed and looked down upon. God has also demonstrated His power and authority to uplift and exalt those who have been abased by the ways of the world. The life of Gideon is a great example of what God can do for those who trust Him! God will choose "the weak things of the world" to confound the mighty and can confuse the wisdom of the world with His infinite wisdom! God bless and much love.

# Daily Devotions

———◇◈◈◇———

Good morning! Read Proverbs 18:21 and Matthew 12:31–37, then John 1:14. We are connected to one another by the words we speak. The words we speak come from the heart. We build up one another and tear down one another by the words we speak to one another. Our words also connect us to God. Our words can condemn us, but it's God's Word that convicts to repentance. We don't conform God to our words, but we conform our lives to the Word of God. God bless and much love.

# Daily Devotions

---

Good morning! Read Isaiah 1:16–19 and Jeremiah 15:16. It's always healthy to wash our hands before we eat. Many love eating at an all-you-can-eat buffet. Having an endless choice of food to choose from. But you must have a plate to put the food on. God has a buffet of blessings for all. But you must have the plate of faith, hope, and trust! You must also wash and make yourself clean. Having washed in the blood of Christ that cleanses us completely that we may enjoy the buffet of blessings God has prepared. God bless and much love.

# Daily Devotions

———◇◈◇———

Good morning! Read 2 Corinthians 4:1–10. It's difficult for anyone to walk in the dark. But with a light, we can see our way clearly. Those who believe in the Gospel of Christ have the light to see clearly in life. But those who don't believe have been blinded by the things of this world and cannot see the Light of Christ. Criticizing and persecuting those who do believe. Although the believer may be cast down by the world, it is God who gives us strength to persevere. To exalt us and lift us in the Light of Christ! God bless and much love.

# Daily Devotions

---

Good morning! Read John 1:18 and 2 Corinthians 4:18, then 1 John 4:11–14. We cannot see the wind, but we feel its effects. We cannot see heat nor cold, but we also feel their effects. We believe them because we feel them; therefore, we know they exist. God has never been seen, but we have seen His effects throughout time. The Holy Spirit is not seen, but we see His effects in our lives when we believe and receive His power into our lives. It's the unseen things of God that are eternal! But you must believe! God bless and much love.

# Daily Devotions

---

Good morning! Read 1 Corinthians 1:25–31. There have been many considered wise and intellectual who have lived throughout history. In fact, there are many self-proclaimed wise and intellectual people living today. However, the wisdom and intellectual thinking of anyone is foolishness in comparison to the wisdom of God! The weakness of God is stronger than anyone and His wisdom is infinite! God's wisdom created everything in this world and beyond! Can anyone else say that? I didn't think so! God bless and much love.

# Daily Devotions

———◇◇◇◇———

Good morning! Read Ecclesiastes 12:13–14. We all have responsibilities of some sort. Whether to our families, our jobs, to each other or most importantly, to ourselves. By fulfilling our responsibilities, we are satisfied and meet the satisfaction of our peers. To fall short of what is expected leaves us feeling incomplete in many ways. Our responsibility to God is to give Him the honor and respect He deserves. By doing so, God will enable us to meet our other responsibilities. But our responsibility to God must be first! God bless and much love.

# Daily Devotions

---

Good morning! Read Jeremiah 2:13 and Hosea 4:6. The more knowledge we have, the better is our understanding and the more understanding increases our knowledge. One complements the other! However, lacking in one is also lacking in the other! A lack in your understanding of God is because of your lack of knowledge of God! We give our time and efforts to know and understand many things! How much time and effort do you give to know and understand God? Time with God is time well spent! God bless and much love.

# Daily Devotions

---

Good morning! Read Matthew 11:28–30 and John 10:10, then 1 Peter 5:8. The devil is always attempting to steal your joy by creating false thoughts in your mind. Often to maximize small things and minimize the larger things that need your immediate attention! Creating stress and anxiety that goes beyond the mental but can have physical effects as well! However, the one sure solution to the devil's poison is found in Christ! Christ is the only antidote to overcome the devil's poison! The cure is found only in Him! God bless and much love.

# Daily Devotions

---

Good morning! Read Job 13:15–18 and Psalm 37:3–6, then Daniel 3:17–18. How much do you trust God? With your entire life or up to a certain point? Receiving the benefits of the blessings of God requires complete commitment to God. Doing anything half-heartedly brings about minimum results. Maximum results require maximum effort! Living a life pleasing to God is putting your life in His hands and trusting Him completely. God bless and much love.

# Daily Devotions

---

Good morning! Read Genesis 1:31 and Psalm 118:24. We often say that "variety is the spice of life"! God has given us a variety in what He has created. The variety in the colors of a rainbow. In the trees and mountains and fish in the seas. Even the stars in the night skies are different as well as each snowflake and raindrop. The color and size in each one of us are different. There are no two people alike. God looked at all He created and said, "It is good!" Let us rejoice each day at what God has created and say, "It is good!" God bless and much love.

# Daily Devotions

———◇◇◇◇◇———

Good morning! Read Isaiah 6:8 and Matthew 5:14–16. God has called His children to go forth throughout the world to speak His Word. Sometimes we must walk alone, yet we are not alone because the Spirit of God goes with us. We are like a candle among candles, showing our light so all may see. If you are the only candle, just remember, the candle that shines alone shines best when it's the only light that can be seen. Especially when that candle carries the Light of God! God bless and much love.

# Daily Devotions

———◆◆◆———

Good morning! Read 2 Corinthians 1:3–4 and Philippians 2:1–5, then James 5:13–20. The more time we spend with someone, the more we get to know them and the more we understand them. If they have evil and wicked tendencies, this is what we learn. If they live with love and compassion, this is what we learn. When we spend time with God, we learn of His *love* and comfort to all who love Him. To put on the characteristics of God so we may be Christlike to all we meet. To provide comfort and prayers to all! God bless and much love.

# Daily Devotions

---

Good morning! Read 1 Corinthians 8:6–13. Mutual respect is showing respect to those that are respectful to you. But the child of God goes further in their respect for others. They show compassion and respect for another's weaknesses as well as their strengths. They are willing to do without so others may have. They are willing to abstain from anything that may be offensive to someone else. Understanding that showing and having respect for someone else is abiding in the will and purpose of God! God bless and much love.

# Daily Devotions

———⬦⬦⬦⬦———

Good morning! Read John 3:3–8 and 2 Corinthians 5:17, then Philippians 2:5. Many want a change in their life. To have a fresh perspective and outlook in what they see and do. The mind is where change begins! A new life must be accompanied by a new way of thinking. You cannot begin a new life with the same old you. Having the mind of Christ makes all things new. But you must be born again! Be free from the old to receive what is new in Christ Jesus. God bless and much love.

# Daily Devotions

---◇◇◇---

Good morning! Read Romans 10:9–13 and 2 Corinthians 5:17. Our confession of Jesus Christ as our Savior opens the door to salvation. To deliver us and separate us from what is to what can be. Most importantly, the salvation of God covers our sins and gives us the strength to resist when we are tempted by sin. Our sin nature can take us from the frying pan into the fire, but the salvation of God cleanses us from sin and gives us a new life in Christ. Replacing the stress and anxiety of this life with the peace of God only God can give. God bless and much love.

# Daily Devotions

---

Good morning! Read Matthew 6:33–34 and John 14:1. Jesus often spoke of the kingdom of God and putting God first! That we not worry but believe that God would provide our every need and to not lose hope. That our emotions and anxieties will be in control as long as we look to God on a daily basis. That the foundation of our heart, soul, mind, and strength be in God who knows all and sees every need that we have. That our heart be not troubled but to believe in Him! To live in His peace! God bless and much love.

# Daily Devotions

———◈◈◈◈◈———

Good morning! Read Jeremiah 29:11–13. Whenever we begin anything, we visualize the completed end. We always feel satisfaction when our purpose has been fulfilled and complete. The tedious work that has been involved is forgotten and seems worthwhile when we see our finished work. We feel the time is well spent upon completion. Our life is visualized in the mind of God. Our work by God in us maybe tedious and difficult at times, but it is worthwhile when we see His finished work in us! God bless and much love.

# Daily Devotions

———◆◇◆◇◆———

Good morning! Read Isaiah 49:16. A song that's widely known refers to God having the whole world in His hands. The children of God have their names and lives graven on the palms of His hands! Every heartbeat and every breath we take is because of the mercy and grace of God! The life we have is because of God's great love He has for us. By losing ourself in God and being filled with the Spirit is where we truly find ourselves. Therefore, let us remain attached to the One who has the whole world in His hands! God bless and much love.

# Daily Devotions

---

Good morning! Read 2 Corinthians 4:1–6. The moment we accept Jesus Christ as our Savior, our lives begin to change. We renounce the hidden things of dishonesty and live as honestly as we can. Receiving the Gospel of Christ readily and willfully! However, there are many whose minds have been blinded by the devil so they cannot see the light of the glorious Gospel of Christ! Therefore, it's important we keep them in prayer until the veil is lifted so the Light of Christ may shine on them! God bless and much love.

# Daily Devotions

———◆◇◆———

Good morning! Read Ecclesiastes 4:9–12 and Amos 3:3, then Micah 6:8 and Romans 8:28. To walk with God, you must be in agreement with God. His thoughts must be your thoughts, and His words must be your words. Walking with God also contains the fullness of the Godhead. This is a wall of protection for us as we are confronted by persecution from the evil around us. Turning what is meant for our harm to what is for our good. God bless and much love.

# Daily Devotions

---◈◈◈◈◈---

Good morning! Read Psalm 119:33–36 and Proverbs 22:6, then John 16:13–14. We are teachers to our children from the time they are born. Helping them to read and write and teaching them right from wrong. When we are born again by the Holy Spirt of God, we are children of God, and God has given us His Spirit to teach us what is right and wrong in the way we live. Always training us as we too train our children that they may not depart but forever have the spiritual tools to live a spiritual life backed by the favor and love of God. God bless and much love.

# Daily Devotions

———⬦⬦⬦———

Good morning! Read John 15:1–12. When we go to the doctor or dentist, their exams are up close and personal. When a tree is pruned, the one doing the cutting must be up close and personal. Even though each instance may cause some pain, the end result is we are much better after their work is done. We put our life in the hands of doctors, dentists, and other professionals but are hesitant to put our life in the hands of God. If we abide in Him, He most certainly will abide in us! Up close and personal! God bless and much love.

# Daily Devotions

———◇◇◇◇◇———

Good morning! Read Joel 2:21–26 and Romans 8:28, then 1 John 4:4. Every blessing that God gives, the devil wants to steal and take it away. But when you firmly believe the promises of God you know and understand that whatever the devil steals and takes away God is able to restore and replace. Because of the promises of God, we are able to maintain our joy in the Lord knowing that all things work together for the good when we love God! It's God in us that overcomes whatever the devil does! God bless and much love.

# Daily Devotions

---

Good morning! Read 2 Chronicles 7:14 and Jonah 3:8–10. The character of God never changes because God never changes. God's mercy, grace and truth endures forever! However, God does change His mind at times in regards of what to allow and what not to allow in our lives. When we are obedient, God can and will withdraw the hand of the evil one from our life. But it's because of our disobedience that the evil one may be allowed to affect our life. If we repent, God will relent and show us His mercy and grace! God bless and much love.

# Daily Devotions

---

Good morning! Read Matthew 7:21–27 and John 14:23–24, then 1 John 2:3–6. There are many who confess and profess Christ but are not obedient to the words of Christ! Being Christlike in their appearance but living a life hypocritical by their actions! Not seriously considering what others can't see and hear that God in Christ sees and hears all! It's so important that if you be in Christ that you do your best to walk even as He walked! To build your spiritual house on His truth and doing your best to live in His truth! God bless and much love.

# Daily Devotions

---

Good morning! Read Proverbs 3:27–29 and Ecclesiastes 4:9–12, then Galatians 6:9–10. It's always good to give to charities and to help those in need. People that we don't know but God knows them just as he knows us. Let's not forget to also help those in need that we do know. Especially those in the household of faith. Just saying "God bless you" and not satisfying their need is really not fulfilling what God wants you to do when it's in your power to do so. God has given to us to bless others so all can be satisfied in all things. God bless and much love.

# Daily Devotions

---

Good morning! Read Psalm 23:1–6 (emphasis on verse 4), then Isaiah 54:17. As we walk through the valley of the shadow of death, we are not to fear anything because God is with us. No matter how big the shadow is, in reality, it can't hurt you. It's only a shadow! The devil uses the shadow to put fear in us. Only when we let the shadow overwhelm us are we defeated. We, in turn, overwhelm the shadow when we put our trust in God. No weapon of the adversary can prosper against us when the weapon of our warfare is God Himself. God bless and much love.

# Daily Devotions

Good morning! Read Colossians 3:1–10. There is much going on in the lives of people we know and in our lives as well. At times life itself can be challenging. But if we are risen with Christ, our eyes are fixed on Him and not on what challenges us. The biggest challenge is to change who we are! To put off our old ways which are the root of our everyday challenges and put on a new way in Christ to meet and overcome the daily challenges that life throws at us. To be renewed in the knowledge of God! God bless and much love.

# Daily Devotions

———◇◇◇◇◇———

Good morning! Read Psalm 12:6 and Colossians 3:15–17, then Hebrews 4:12. It's wise to be careful of the words we speak. When our words have gone forth, we cannot bring them back. Therefore, we should choose our words wisely. Our words can be a blessing and comfort those in need or be a curse and be offensive to others. However, if the Word of God is the "center point" of our life we will be wise in the words we speak. Let the Word of God reside in you that you may be a blessing in your spoken words! God bless and much love.

# Daily Devotions

---

Good morning! Read 1 Corinthians 6:9–11 and 2 Corinthians 5:10. The mercy and forgiveness of God *should* lead us to repentance! To give us a change of heart and mind to adopt a new life in Christ. Unfortunately, there are some who use God's mercy and forgiveness as a liberty to continue living a way of life not pleasing to God because He is forgiving. Not understanding we will be judged according to the things we have done, whether it be good or bad. Therefore, repent that your works are pleasing to God! God bless and much love.

# Daily Devotions

---

Good morning! Read 1 Timothy 6:5–12. Many live their lives in an effort to accumulate as much wealth as they can. Not understanding we brought nothing into this world, and it is certain we can carry nothing out! However, it's living a godly life that is the greatest gain! But the love of money and wealth have caused many to error and turn away from their faith! It's so important we stay the course and fight the good fight of faith! Wealth in this life is temporary! The things of God are eternal! God bless and much love.

# Daily Devotions

---◇◈◇◈◇---

Good morning! Read Psalm 73:25–28. When two pieces of cloth are knit together, the two become one piece. For those that love God, it is our desire to have our heart knit together with the heart of God. To see as God sees and have the love and understanding that God has. Being humbled knowing we are forever in the presence of God. Without God, we are like a piece of cloth torn away from the main piece. We become useless until we are knitted back together to again become a part of the whole. God bless and much love.

# Daily Devotions

---

Good morning! Read Matthew 4:4 and John 1:1–4, then Romans 5:17–21. One question that has baffled mankind is "Which came first, the chicken or the egg?" The answer is neither! The beginning of all things began with the Word of God! It's His Word that was spoken that created all things, and it's every word of His Word that we should live by. It's sin that keeps us from His Word, but it's His Word that cleanses and keeps us from sin. Although to sin can be tempting at times, the grace and strength of God is greater! God bless and much love.

# Daily Devotions

———◇◆◇———

Good morning! Read Jude verses 20–25. Whenever a building is rebuilt, it must first be torn down and demolished. New construction must be done with new materials that are strong enough to last. A new life in Christ requires us to destroy and demolish the old life. The new materials in building a new life requires our most holy faith and trust in the builder who is God! Looking to God who is able to keep us from falling. That we may be faultless in His presence. God is the Master Builder! God bless and much love.

# Daily Devotions

———◆◈◆◈◆———

Good morning! Read John 16:13–15. It's always wise to be sensitive and pay attention to detail in everything we do. Paying attention to detail gives us understanding to what we see and hear. It's also important to be sensitive and pay attention to the voice of the Holy Spirit! It's the Holy Spirit of God that speaks to our spirit to give us guidance and direction daily in our life. When we pay attention to the detail of the Holy Spirit, God is glorified, and we are glorified in God! But you must have a listening ear! God bless and much love.

# Daily Devotions

⬥⬥⬥⬥⬥

Good morning! Read Deuteronomy 13:1–7 and Acts 19:18–20. There are many who seek those with "curious arts," such as psychics, astrologers, card or palm readers, fortune tellers, etc. This is part of the devil's persuasion to sway you away from God. To entice you into a demonic and false hope with false promises! It's important for you to withstand and withdraw from this and anything else that would create an open door for you to be tempted! The temptations of the tempter will be overcome by your strength in God! God bless and much love.

# Daily Devotions

---

Good morning! Read Hebrews 11:6 and James 2:14–18 and 26. Many speak of having faith in God and wanting to grow in their faith. However, having true faith and growing in true faith requires you to put your faith into action! To take steps of faith daily that you may grow daily in faith! Our faith is demonstrated by the faithful works we do in faith more than merely speaking of our faith! It's said, the proof is in the pudding! True faith is proved by working out your faith by taking daily steps of faith! God bless and much love.

# Daily Devotions

---

Good morning! Read Luke 15:11–32. God has given us His gift of grace. His grace never departs from us, but we sometimes depart from His grace. Allowing ourselves to be lured into a lifestyle out of God's will doing things according to our own. But be thankful to God for always giving us another chance and helping us to get back on course that leads us back to Him. God's grace is sufficient to help us repent and reestablish ourselves into His loving arms and care. God's love for us never changes. God bless and much love.

# Daily Devotions

———◇◆◇◆◇———

Good morning! Read Revelation 20:12–15. When we make a reservation, our name is written down. When we arrive at the time of our reservation, our name is found, and we can enter because we have a place reserved. To have a reservation in the Book of Life, we have to make a reservation. We reserve our name by accepting Jesus Christ as our Savior. By Him, we have a reservation for life eternally in the presence with God. Without *that* reservation, the best life you will live is the one you're living now. Make the reservation! God bless and much love.

# Daily Devotions

———◇◇◇◇◇———

G ood morning! Read 2 Corinthians 10:3–7 and James 1:13–17. We all face some type of temptation every day. The question is do you succumb to the temptation or do you rise above it? Although we live in the flesh, we must be spiritually minded to rise above the weakness of the flesh. To cast down every thought that goes against the knowledge we have of God that we may be obedient to His Word. Looking with hope to receive that good and perfect gift that comes down from our Father in heaven! God bless and much love.

# Daily Devotions

---

Good morning! Read Matthew 13:3–9 and 18–23. Whenever we plant a seed, it's important we plant the seed in fertile ground. We must water the seed for the seed to grow. We must also protect the seed from excessive heat and cold. We can't neglect the seed when we are busy or during stressful times for it to grow. The seed of the Word of God must be planted in the fertile ground of our heart. We must nourish it the same way we would for any plant. Only then can we receive the fruits of the Word! God bless and much love.

# Daily Devotions

---

Good morning! Read John 14:6 and Ephesians 4:4–7. There are many beliefs and denominations of faith that have drawn many. Deceiving many in their pursuit to God saying there is more than one way to God. This is contrary to God's Word! Whatever path you are on, that path must lead you to Christ to be lead to God! Jesus Christ is our Lord, and our faith is in the faith of Jesus Christ, and we are baptized in the name of Jesus Christ! Christ is the only way, the truth, and the life that leads to God! God bless and much love.

# Daily Devotions

---

Good morning! Read Isaiah 26:3–4 and Psalm 118:24. We all long to have that perfect day where everything goes right! Where our daily plans all fall into place. Although many may not experience that perfect day, all can experience having God's perfect peace throughout their day when their mind is stayed on God! It's by putting your daily plans into God's hands and trusting God's direction as you go about your day. Rejoicing and thanking God for His perfect peace throughout the day! God bless and much love.

# Daily Devotions

———◆◇◆◇◆———

Good morning! Read Acts 2:38–47. We receive remission of our sins when we repent and believe on Jesus Christ. To be born again in the blood shed by Christ for the forgiveness and the remission of our sins. To receive the doctrine of God found in His Word that saves all who come to Him. To have all things in common with the fellowship of all who believe. God knows the sincerity of all who come to Him and daily adds to His church all who should be saved! Are you among those He has chosen? God bless and much love.

# Daily Devotions

---

Good morning! Read Matthew 6:33 and 11:28–30, then 2 Corinthians 1:3–7. We look to be comforted when we are facing struggles. When life is a seemingly uphill battle. If it's our health, we seek a physician. If it's our finances or family, we seek the counsel of professionals. But God says, "Look unto Me!" Trust God to direct you to the right doctors or professionals for what is best for you in all circumstances. God knows your struggles, and God knows your pain. All God ask is that you seek Him first! God bless and much love.

# Daily Devotions

———◆◇◆◇◆———

Good morning! Read Deuteronomy 28:1–10. God honors and blesses those that are obedient and honor Him. God opens up the widows of blessings and will shut the windows that the curses may not enter. God opens the door to allow His blessings in and shuts the door to keep the curses out. The curse can enter when we open that window or door by disobeying God. God's yes means yes, and His no means no! To honor God is to honor His Word! There are no shortcuts or excuses. Receive His blessings and not the curse. God bless and much love.

# Daily Devotions

———◆◇◆◇◆———

G ood morning! Read 1 Corinthians 1:10–13 and Ephesians 4:4–6. There is much division in the world today, much based on political views, racial ethnicity, likes, dislikes, etc. Sadly, there is much division in the Body of Christ! Many groups or religious denominations believing they are the true religion. The Body of Christ is not whole when it is divided. It's God's will that we be whole in body, soul, and spirit. After all, there is one Lord, Jesus Christ! One faith, also in Jesus Christ! And one baptism which is of the Holy Spirit! God bless and much love.

# Daily Devotions

———◆❖◆———

G ood morning! Read Psalm 46:1–7 and 10, then Isaiah 26:3–4 and Hebrews 13:8. The world is ever changing with more earthquakes, stronger storms, and widespread problems among societies. Violence between nations, states, cities, and our communities. However, although the world is changing, our God does not! God is the same yesterday, today, and forever! It's because of His never changing nature we can find peace in Him in the midst of an ever-changing world! God bless and much love.

# Daily Devotions

---

Good morning! Read John 17:14–20. Although you are in the world, you are no longer of the world when you are sanctified by the truth of the Word of God. The Word of God is bread to the hungry and quenches the thirst of the thirsty! It's the fulfillment of the heart and soul to all who indulge in its truth! The Word of God opens your eyes that you may see the things of this world that has held you back and the things of God that will lead you into a bright and promising future! A future living in God's blessings! God bless and much love.

# Daily Devotions

---

Good morning! Read 1 Corinthians 12:12–27. Our body parts have various functions—eyes to see, ears to hear, the nose to smell, etc. Our inward parts such as the heart, lungs, stomach, etc., have their designed functions as well. Each designed with a specific purpose in the functioning of the body. We are the Body of Christ! We all have different functions, and we must do our part to grow within the Body of Christ! No matter how small or great your part may be, you are important to the building of the Body of Christ! God bless and much love.

# Daily Devotions

———◇◇◇◇◇———

Good morning! Read Proverbs 4:23. There are times when your mind will pull you one way and your heart will pull you another. Creating a conflict within because your heart and mind are not in alignment with one another. If your heart is centered on the things of God, you will have the strength to defeat the wrong thoughts that are generated in the mind. It's important to have your heart and mind in alignment together so what you feel is what you think and what you think is what you feel! God bless and much love.

# Daily Devotions

———◇◈◇———

Good morning! Read Philippians 4:11–13. Having the mindset to do the right things and to resist the wrong things is behavior that is learned over time as we grow and mature. Learning to be content in living a godly lifestyle is also learned over time. It's through the experience of growing in Christ that we learn to be content in good times and in times that don't seem favorable at the time. However, it's knowing Christ is our strength that strengthens us to overcome all things to be content in all things! God bless and much love.

# Daily Devotions

---◇◇◇◇◇---

Good morning! Read Joel 2:25 and John 17:22–23, then 1 Corinthians 3:16–17. We feel a need to protect that which we love and cherish. Whether it's our spouse or children or something having sentimental value. If it's somehow lost, we go to great lengths to find and recover it. God protects what He loves and cherishes also, and He loves and cherishes those who love Him. Whatever we've lost, God is more than able to restore. Our faith activates God's willingness, and He is faithful to all that put their trust in Him. God bless and much love.

# Daily Devotions

———◇◇◇◇◇———

Good morning! Read Luke 6:27–28 and Romans 12:17–21. There are some people we all know that are selfish, uncaring, unappreciative, and not thoughtful of anyone but themselves. Often we have to bite our tongue to keep from acting out or saying what's on our mind. During these times, our best solution is to think and meditate on the Word of God. These types of people need prayer, not retaliation. They need God's mercy and grace to open their eyes to see themselves as they are seen by others. Bottom line, they need God! God bless and much love.

# Daily Devotions

———◇◇◇◇◇◇———

Good morning! Read Genesis 1:11–12 and Proverbs 4:23, then 2 Timothy 1:7. When God created everything, everything was to multiply after its kind, whose seed was in itself. This principle is also a spiritual principle as well. The seeds of fear bring about more fear. Negative thinking brings more negativity. It's also true that faith is the springboard to more faith and love multiplies into more love. Whether for the better or for the worse, the starting point is what is in the heart. Its truth is your truth! God bless and much love.

# Daily Devotions

---

Good morning! Read Matthew 7:24–27. Whenever a house is built, it's important that the foundation is strong and sturdy for the house to last. A weak foundation will cause the house to collapse and fall after time. Unless our spiritual house is founded on the rock of Christ, it will also collapse and fall after time. It's the Word of God that strengthens our spiritual house and maintains us to withstand all the elements of life that we may face in life. It's this foundation built on the rock of Christ that will last! God bless and much love.

# Daily Devotions

---

Good morning! Read Matthew 12:46–50 and John 4:23–24, then James 1:22–25. The true worshippers of God and followers of Christ will readily hear the Word of God and are doers of the Word. It's not a compromising or part time effort but a striving for perfection in Christ Jesus. The true worshippers of God are strong in faith in the promises of God! The true worshippers of God focus their life on doing the will of God and not their own! Are you a true worshipper of God in spirit and in truth? God bless and much love.

# Daily Devotions

---

Good morning! Read Exodus 16:18 and 2 Corinthians 8:12–15. There is much discrepancy between the rich and the poor, between those who have and those who have not. The scales of balance are out of balance! Out of balance by greed and selfishness and the lack of care and love for one another! Many seeking to pleasure themselves rather than pleasing and obeying God's plan of equality! It's only by following God's plan of equality that the scales of balance can be equally balanced! God bless and much love.

# Daily Devotions

———◈◈◈◈◈———

Good morning! Read 1 Corinthians 9:24–27. Conditioning is important for every athlete in preparation for their chosen profession. Maintaining that conditioning throughout the season is vital to their success. Sometimes it's difficult, but having a winning goal gives them reason to keep going. Spiritual conditioning is important as we run this race in life to overcome and win the prize that awaits us at the end. Being deliberate, ensuring our conditioning causes us to win, knowing the victory is in Christ Jesus. God bless and much love.

# Daily Devotions

———◇◇◇◇◇———

Good morning! Read Job 1:21 and Matthew 5:3–12. A common saying is a verse taken from the Book of Job, how "the Lord gives and the Lord takes away." The truth is, this is what Job said, not God. God doesn't take away what He gives. But God gives us a blessing and takes away the curse. God gives us healing and takes away sickness. God gives us peace and takes away confusion. God gives us joy and takes away sorrow. God gives us love and takes away hate. God gives us eternal life and takes away death. Praise Him! God bless and much love.

# Daily Devotions

---

Good morning! Read James 1:22–25. Often many will hear the Word of God preached but fail to apply what they hear into their lives. The power in the word is activated by taking the action of applying it in our lives. By only hearing and not applying is like sitting in a car expecting to go somewhere without starting the engine. It takes action on our part so God can bless us with His part! By only hearing we soon forget, but when we apply what we hear, we reap what the word has sown! God bless and much love.

# Daily Devotions

———◇◇◇◇◇———

Good morning! Read Ephesians 4:11–16. The children of God are somewhat like an orchestra or symphony and God is the conductor, giving direction to each section and each one of us to harmonize and make sweet spiritual music in our lives that can be heard and witnessed to all that see and hear. That our lives may be perfected for the ministry, for the edifying of the Body of Christ! However, we must be in harmony with one another to produce the sweet spiritual sounds of God! God bless and much love.

# Daily Devotions

---

Good morning! Read Acts 4:12 and 16:29–31. We all have sinned and need a savior. To forgive us from our sins and cleanse us from all unrighteousness. To give us a new life and a new start in life. To close the door to the past and open a new door to a new and restored hope for a brighter future. There is only one name in heaven above and on earth that can give us the salvation needed, and that name is Jesus Christ! It by believing on and in the name of Jesus Christ that we are saved! Save yourself in Christ! God bless and much love.

# Daily Devotions

---

Good morning! Read Philippians 4:4–13 and 2 Timothy 1:7. Each day we have a choice of how we want to live that day. We can choose to live it in fear or live it in faith. To expect the worse or to expect the best. To be negative or positive about what the day may bring. Without God, there is skepticism allowing doubt. Opening the door for the spirit of fear to enter. With God, there is hope based on faith which allows the Spirit and power of God to reveal itself in you which shapes your day. Be strong in the power of God! God bless and much love.

# Daily Devotions

———◇◈◇◈◇———

Good morning! Read Jeremiah 18:1–6 and 29:11–13. Every builder and artist has a vision of their finished and completed work, patiently taking each step. Some of which can be painstaking at times until their vision becomes a reality. God builds and shapes our lives step by step. Some of which can be painstaking but necessary for us. Allowing God to complete His work in us is possible when we keep our life in His hands and our heart open to receive His direction. God will finish and complete what He has begun. God bless and much love.

# Daily Devotions

---◇◇◇◇---

Good morning! Read Romans 6:23 and 8:1–6, then Galatians 5:16. God has given us free will to choose. The most important choice we can make is whether we want to live according to the spirit or to live according to the flesh. One leads to life and one leads to death. By living in the spirit, there is no condemnation but by living in the flesh, you are condemned already. The peace of God comes to all that live and walk in the spirit. Any other way will leave you separated from God. What's your choice? God bless and much love.

# Daily Devotions

———◇◇◇———

Good morning! Read Psalm 139:1–12. There is nothing hid from God! There is no corner in our life so dark that He cannot see. There is no thought that He cannot hear nor any feeling in our heart that He does not understand. God is all and in all! Nothing escapes from God's knowing! It's God who leads us when we put our life in His hands. God will lead us through the dark places of life with His guiding light. What is unknown to us is known to God. Place you trust and faith in God who knows all! God bless and much love.

# Daily Devotions

---

Good morning! Read Psalm 27:1 and 91:1–5, then 1 John 4:4. When God is the light of your salvation, you are drawn to His light! It's in the Light of God that we find refuge and peace when we abide under the shadow of the Almighty! Our fears, doubts, and worries are replaced by faith, hope, and trust! Understanding and knowing God is there to deliver us from all the evil the world sends our way! Having the confidence in God in Christ in us to prevail and stand tall through all adversity! God bless and much love.

# Daily Devotions

———◇◇◇◇◇———

Good morning! Read Ecclesiastes 9:4–6 and Luke 9:23–27. When we are born, we know we will someday die. In Christ Jesus, the day we die to ourself we begin to live. When anything dies, it is completely dead. Every thought and every feeling is gone. It is completely empty of what it was. We must be completely empty of ourselves to be born again unto God in Christ. No one likes to drink out of a dirty glass or eat off a dirty plate. Get rid of the scraps in your life and completely die to self that you may begin a new life in Christ. God bless and much love.

# Daily Devotions

———◇◇◇◇◇◇———

Good morning! Read 2 Corinthians 10:3–6 and James 1:12–17. There are many things that influence our way of thinking. What we see and hear on social media or television or the music we listen to can affect our thoughts. Our thoughts can shape and mold who we become if we are not wise in our selection process of what we allow to influence us. Much can be appealing but can ruin our life if we allow the wrong things to enter and change who we are destined to be. But God can give us the wisdom to choose wisely when our foundation is in Him. God bless and much love.

# Daily Devotions

---

Good morning! Read 1 Corinthians 2:9–16. Whenever we encounter someone that speaks a different language, we need an interpreter to understand what they're saying. Without an interpreter, we can't understand them, and neither can they understand us. Only by living in the spirit can we understand the spiritual things of God. To those living in the natural, it is like an unknown language without an interpreter. They have no understanding! The Holy Spirit is the interpreter to all living in the Spirit! God bless and much love.

# Daily Devotions

———◇◆◇◆◇———

Good morning! Read 1 Corinthians 2:9–16. The spiritual things of God that are revealed to the children of God are confusing and not understood by those who don't believe or those who don't know God. It's like hearing a foreign language they don't understand. Only those with a godly spirit have understanding of the spiritual ways of God. Only those with a godly spirit can compare spiritual things with what's spiritual and have understanding. Do you have spiritual understanding of the ways of God? God bless and much love.

# Daily Devotions

———◆◆◆———

G ood morning! Read 1 Samuel 16:7 and Romans 12:1–2. We can change our outward appearance to impress and appeal to others. From head to toe, we are able to change our outward appearance to create the image we want. However, it's the inward person of the heart that impresses and appeals to God! A heart that is not conformed to this world but has been transformed by the renewing of the mind to prove what is good and acceptable and perfect in the eyes of God! Do you need a changed heart? God bless and much love.

# Daily Devotions

---

Good morning! Read Matthew 5:18 and 1 Peter 1:24–25, then Revelation 21:22–27. There is nothing that we can taste, touch, smell, or see that will not one day fade away. Even our body, that is our home in this life, will one day perish. Only the voice of God we hear in the spirit of our heart will last. Only God is eternal and those written in the Book of Life will be forever with God. This life we live is temporary. Just a small moment in time. God is timeless and so too are those whose names are written in the Book of Life! God bless and much love.

# Daily Devotions

---

Good morning! Read Matthew 4:17 and Acts 4:12, then Romans 10:9–13. Jesus Christ came into the world to save the world. Preaching the kingdom of God that all who believed would be saved. This saving grace is in His name and in His name alone! It's the believing in the power and saving grace in His name that we are saved. Believing begins in the heart unto the righteousness of Christ and we testify and confess our hope and faith in His name! It is the only road to salvation! God bless and much love.

# Daily Devotions

---

Good morning! Read Luke 2:46–49 and Philippians 2:5. As children, we always watched our parents and often tried to emulate what they were doing, trying to be like daddy and mommy. We were always about their business. As a child, Jesus was all about his Father's business! Giving us the example to follow in learning the business of God! When we put on the mind of Christ, we also will be about the Father's business. Have you put on the mind of Christ? Are you about the Father's business? God bless and much love.

# Daily Devotions

---

G ood morning! Read Genesis 1:26–28. There are many who believe in the theory of evolution and reject the truth of God's creation. Believing we evolved from monkeys or some other species. If that were true, why do monkeys and other species still exist? The only evolution that applies to the child of God is that of spiritual evolution! That our spiritual life evolves from believing to having faith to stronger faith! From having hope to greater hope and trust to greater trust in God! God bless and much love.

# Daily Devotions

———◆◆◆◆◆———

Good morning! Read James 1:5–9. Bad days can become worst days when our days are lived in hopelessness. But good days can become better days when we live each day having faith in the wisdom of God that God freely gives to all who ask! However, godly wisdom is received by having complete faith in God! Partial faith is like drinking a glass of water without the glass! You need the glass to hold the water and you need faith to hold the wisdom of God! Make every day a good day by living in the wisdom of God! God bless and much love.

# Daily Devotions

———◇◇◇◇◇———

Good morning! Read Romans 12:1–2 and 14:7–13. It's easy to run with the crowd. To be accepted and be in good standing with them. At times doing what we know in our heart is wrong. To be seen as being cool to all that know us and see us. It's harder to run with the things of God who we have not seen but sees our every move and knows our every thought. To be accepted by God should be our number one priority. Your friends with change but God never will. It's His judgment that counts and not that of your friends. God bless and much love.

# Daily Devotions

———◆◇◆◇◆———

Good morning! Read Matthew 26:41 and Ephesians 6:18, then Philippians 4:6–7. God is all knowing. He knows the hearts and minds of each of us. Some may ask, "If God knows all, why is there a need to pray?" Prayer is not only for God but for us. It opens the door of our innermost being whereby we are in touch with who we really are. But it's the prayer of faith with all sincerity that moves God. We only know ourselves when we expose ourselves to ourselves. It's what separates the flesh from the spirit within. Having a spiritual hunger for the Spirit of God. God bless and much love.

# Daily Devotions

———◆◈◆———

Good morning! Read 2 Corinthians 6:14–18. You cannot mix oil with water. Neither would you plant a garden in a bed of weeds. You first clear the soil and cultivate the ground so the garden will grow. You then water the garden as needed. In this life, the children of God are the garden of God, and the unbelievers are the weeds. God has sanctified us and watered us with His Spirit. Like any garden, when weeds appear, they must be removed, or they will choke what's growing. How are *you* growing? God bless and much love.

# Daily Devotions

---

Good morning! Read Matthew 7:15–20. There is much deception in the world today. Inside the Christian community and outside of the Christian community, there are those who are set on deceiving others for their personal gain. But those who are wise in the wisdom of God will recognize these wolves in sheep's clothing! A good person will speak in honesty of good things, but a corrupt person has a hidden agenda! Know and understand so you are not deceived by the deceiver! God bless and much love.

# Daily Devotions

---◇⬩◇⬩◇---

Good morning! Read Psalm 37:3–9 and 23–24. When we commit our life to God, we are proving our trust in God. To walk and live according to God's Word in faith and hope. Believing God will meet the desires of our heart when we are ready to receive them. Patiently waiting as God prepares our steps daily to walk the path of life that leads us closer to Him. Although we may fall at times, God is there to lift us up and give us the strength to maintain and carry on in our endeavor to live a life pleasing to Him! God bless and much love.

# Daily Devotions

———◇◈◇———

Good morning! Read Deuteronomy 30:15–19 and Joshua 24:14–15. God has given all an opportunity of free will to choose the type of life they wish to live. To live according to His will or our own. God's will is obedience to His word which can open doors that no one can shut and can shut doors that can bring us hurt, pain, suffering, and even death. We are blindly led by our own will. Not knowing nor understanding the severity of the choices we make. A short-term fix may have lasting consequences. The best counsel comes from God. God bless and much love.

# Daily Devotions

---

Good morning! Read John 8:29 and Romans 10:13 and 12:1–2. Everyone has envisioned a life they want to live. A life without any worries or feeling pressure of any kind. A simple life but rewarding in every aspect. The life you want is the life God wants you to have. The first step is to lay aside the life you've been living and commit yourself to living a godly life. A life that is pleasing to God and God is pleased with your life. Doing God's will brings assurance and satisfaction to the life you desire to live when God's will becomes your will. God bless and much love.

# Daily Devotions

———◇◇◇◇◇———

Good morning! Read Mark 9:23–24 and Hebrews 4:9–12 and 11:6. God has given us many promises in His Word. Promises that can bring rest to all who believe. But it's because of unbelief that keep the promises of God from being fulfilled in the lives of many. Our faith is based on what we believe, and it's our faith in the promises of God that bring His promises to pass. Only by knowing God's Word do you learn the promises of God. Only then can you declare and claim them in your life through your faith in Him! God bless and much love.

# Daily Devotions

———◇◈◇———

G ood morning! Read Psalm 138:2. Our
peers know we are reliable when we keep
our word. The keeping of our word shows our
integrity and dignity we have for ourselves.
The saying "my word is my bond" is important to us and our honesty speaks volumes to
our peers. The words God has spoken to us in
His Word speaks volumes about the honesty
and integrity of God. God's sees His Word as
being more important than His name. The
promises of God are flawless, and we can rely
on Him to keep His Word! God bless and
much love.

# Daily Devotions

---

Good morning! Read Matthew 6:31–34. God is righteous, and for us to wear the cloak of righteousness of God, we must be right with God! We must seek God first in the waking hours of each day. We must show our love and appreciation for God and what He has done in our life. Understand it's not our strength but the strength of God that strengthens us to overcome the trials we face daily. God knows our weaknesses and our needs. We need God every hour of every day! Seek Him first! God bless and much love.

# Daily Devotions

———◆◇◆◇◆———

G ood morning! Read Isaiah 6:8 and Luke 10:1–12. What we have heard and learned of the good things of God we should share with those around us. That their lives may be enhanced by God the way ours has been. God is looking for those to do this very thing! God sent Jesus and Jesus shared and sent the message of the Gospel through those who believed in Him! God in Christ through the Holy Spirit is now sending us! However, you must know the message of the gospel to share the gospel! Do you? God bless and much love.

# Daily Devotions

---◈◈◈◈◈---

Good morning! Read Isaiah 9:2 and John 1:6–9, then Revelation 21:23. When we stand in front of a light, we cast a shadow. The brighter the light, the deeper and broader the shadow. A shadow of our image that goes with us while we are in the light. When we stand before God whose light is far greater than the sun, we also cast a shadow. But this image is not of us but of God in Christ in us that we reflect for the world to see. Knowing that even though we walk in a darkened world we have the Light of God to lead the way. God bless and much love.

# Daily Devotions

---

Good morning! Read 2 Corinthians 4:3–4 and 2 Thessalonians 2:8–12, then 1 Timothy 4:1–2. We are living in an age where those spirited by the evil ones are trying to discredit the Word of God. Choosing to believe a lie than the truth of the Bible. Being critical without any understanding of what the Bible is all about. The Bible not only prophesied but foretold that these days would come. Proving again of its truth! Those who reject the Word are blinded through belief. Living a darkened life that cannot see the light of the glorious Gospel of Christ! God bless and much love.

# Daily Devotions

———✦✦✦———

Good morning! Read Psalm 23:1–6 and 3rd John verse 2. There are many that go through hard times, and many are going through hard times at this moment. Often God allows hard times in our life because it's through hard times that lead us to Him. Only then do we see and can appreciate what the will of God is for us. His will is that we prosper in our life by having prosperity in our health, body, and soul. This prosperity begins with having a spiritual relationship with God. It's through His Spirit that we are made whole! God bless and much love.

# Daily Devotions

---

Good morning! Read Psalm 23:3–4 and Proverbs 16:9, then Galatians 5:16. When we allow the Spirit of God to lead us it will lead us in the way we need to go. To the doorway of God's blessings and away from the door of destruction! It will lead us to the right people and away from those that will hinder our journey. However, we must keep our eyes and ears open to what the Spirit says and see the direction that we are being led and allow the Spirit of God to direct your way! God bless and much love.

# Daily Devotions

———◇◇◇◇◇◇———

Good morning! Read Isaiah 45:18 and Colossians 1:12–19. When we behold the beauty of the heavens in the night skies, we see the glory of God's creation. The oceans, streams, mountains, trees, etc., also proclaim God's glory. Everything God has created has a purpose, and there is a plan to His purpose! From the smallest creation to the greatest, there is a plan and purpose! There is a plan and purpose in God's mind for you and me. God has given us life that we may have life in Him through His Son Jesus Christ! God bless and much love.

# Daily Devotions

---

Good morning! Read Genesis 39:1–4 and 20–23, then 2 Corinthians 6:4–10. We live in a world that's hurting with hurt people hurting other people. Lost in hopelessness searching for peace that eludes their every effort. With the children of God, there is hope. God's favor is with us even when cast down by our peers. The life of Joseph is a great example of this. He was sold into slavery by his brothers and imprisoned by Pharaoh. God showed him favor, and he prospered to becoming governor over the land. Trust God and His favor. God bless and much love.

# Daily Devotions

———◇◆◇◆◇———

Good morning! Read Exodus 20:17 and 2 Corinthians 10:12–18, then Colossians 3:1–4. The Tenth Commandment is "Thou shalt not covet." Yet many look and compare themselves to others. Seeking and searching the approval of their peers. Often stretching beyond their means to one up someone else. Not understanding that the only approval that really matters is the approval of God. If you're going to compare, compare yourself with the one in the mirror. Does your reflection meet your

# Daily Devotions

---

Good morning Read Isaiah 59:1 and Lamentations 3:19–26, then Romans 10:13. We all face times when everything seems to be going wrong. We often wonder why this is happening when we're doing all we can to live right. Feeling lonely and that God is at a distance and our situations can't be helped. But we must always keep in mind that God's hand is not shortened that it cannot save and that He hears us when we call! Because of His mercies we are not consumed. God is our relief and our hope! God bless and much love.

# Daily Devotions

———◇◈◇———

Good morning! Read 2 Corinthians 12:7–10. There are times when it seems our prayers are unanswered. When our prayers seem to fall short of what we feel we need. But we must remember and recall to our mind that it's the strength and power of God that carries us at our weakest point. There is always a lesson learned during these times of unanswered prayer! That it's His strength that is made perfect during our times of weakness and it's His grace that is sufficient in all things! God bless and much love.

# Daily Devotions

———◈◈◈———

Good morning! Read 2 Corinthians 12:7–10 and Philippians 4:5–7, then 1 Peter 5:6–11. Trying to carry the weight of the world on our shoulders can be burdensome and tiring. Slowly drawing our strength and leaving us in a weakened state of mind. However, it's through our weakness that the strength and power of Christ is perfected in us! It's by humbling ourselves before God and putting our cares and concerns in His hands that we are strengthened with new life in Christ! God bless and much love.

# Daily Devotions

———✦———

G ood morning! Read 1 Samuel 16:7 and Matthew 13:3–9 and 16–23. Whenever we buy a car, we are first attracted by the outward appearance. We check the engine to make sure we're not buying a lemon. We use the proper gas, oil, and spark plugs to ensure long life. After all, the engine is the heart of the car. God sees our heart first. He checks our heart and not our outward appearance to ensure that we have long life. But the maintenance is our responsibility. God can take you as a lemon and make lemonade. God bless and much love.

# Daily Devotions

———◈◈◈◈◈———

G ood morning! Read Proverbs 3:7–8 and 16:18, then Romans 1:20–25. One of the biggest downfalls of anyone is pride. When anyone is full of pride, there is little or no room for God. Instead of seeking to be led by God, they chose to lead themselves. The blind leading the blind. Being prideful in their own wisdom and ignoring the wisdom of God. This prideful mindset leads to eventual destruction to not only that person but those around them feel the effects as well. It's so important to empty ourselves of ourselves to be filled with the goodness and wisdom of God. God bless and much love.

# Daily Devotions

———◇◆◇◆◇———

Good morning! Read Malachi 1:6–9 and Mark 12:29–31. Whenever we give a gift to a loved one, family member, or friend, we choose something we know they will like. We give them the best of the best that we can afford. However, many give God what's left. The last fruits instead of the first fruits, so to speak. In truth, God doesn't need anything because all things belong to Him. What God desires most is *you*! That you seek Him with all your heart, soul, mind, and strength! In this, God is well pleased! God bless and much love.

# Daily Devotions

G ood morning! Read Luke 9:23–26. True followers of Christ live their life by putting God first on a daily basis. It's more than just a once or twice a week of fellowship and worship. It's a continued daily worship and fellowship with the Holy Spirit of God. It's being bold in our confession of Christ by the words we speak on His behalf. It's not being ashamed of our profession of Christ but the giving of our life completely to Him. To die to ourselves and to live unto Him! To save our life by losing it in Christ Jesus! God bless and much love.

# Daily Devotions

———◈✦◈———

Good morning! Read Nehemiah 8:10 and Isaiah 26:3–4. Everyone has a desire to live a peaceful and joyful life. To be shielded from the problems of stress and worries of everyday life. To be open and free to receive the good things life has to offer. To the wise, God is that joy and God is that peace! Having the joy of the Lord as their strength in living a joyful life and having their trust in God as their everlasting strength! It's important that your mind be stayed on God to receive His joy and His peace! God bless and much love.

# Daily Devotions

———◇◇◇◇◇———

Good morning! Read Mark 13:5–10 and 19–23. There are many that are shaken and express surprise at the continued onslaught of the world's problems. Increasing unrest among the nations and more severe weather conditions and the increase of violence in our schools and society. But those who know and understand the Word of God are not surprised! Everything happening in the world today was foretold thousands of years ago. It's so important to prepare ourselves for the coming day of the Lord! God bless and much love.

# Daily Devotions

---

Good morning! Read Mark 11:22–24. Receiving the desires of your heart begins with seeing your desires come to pass by having the belief that God will make it happen if it's according to His will. However, our desires require having a plan that leads to its completion. It must be a sustained desire and belief having a vision of the desired result. Having faith in God is the hope of His fulfillment of the desire that's in your heart. It's by first believing that opens up the doors to receive! We walk through the doors by having faith! God bless and much love.

# Daily Devotions

---

Good morning! Read Micah 7:7–10 and 1 Peter 3:12–17. Our God is the God of our salvation. God hears our prayers, and it's with patience that we wait on Him. Even when we fall, it is God who will raise us up. Despite what we may hear or see from those around us, it is the strength we receive from the Spirit of God that sustains us. Although it may be darkness in the lives of others, our God is the Light to light our way that we may see His righteousness and be delivered. The doubters will be shamed but we will be rewarded! God bless and much love.

# Daily Devotions

---

Good morning! Read Luke 14:28–35 and 18:27, then John 16:13–14. When we look at any challenge, we always consider the risk, weighing the odds of success. When we put our trust in God, His wisdom will guide us in our decision making. Only God can make the impossible possible. God's direction is the best direction even though we may not see or understand. It's our trust and faith that God uses to light the way and lead us to where we need to be. That we may be encouraged and not discouraged in our efforts. God bless and much love.

# Daily Devotions

---◇◈◇---

Good morning! Read Matthew 6:9–13 and 26:39–42, then John 5:30 and 1 John 4:4. Prayer and praise and the giving of thanks are essential to the child of God. It is the starting point to growing our faith. Releasing our will and submitting to the will of God. That the will of God be done on earth, as it is in heaven. Living our life according to His heavenly calling that we may be complete in all things pertaining to life and godliness. Powered by the Holy Spirit and overcoming anything that may cause us to stumble. God bless and much love.

# Daily Devotions

———◇◇◇◇◇———

Good morning! Read Hebrews 11:6. Often to get from one mountain across to the other side, a bridge must be crossed. We also may have to cross a bridge to pass over a body of water to get to the other side. There is also a bridge that must be crossed to go from unbelief to believing in the things of God! It's the bridge of faith you must cross that leads you from faith to faith in God through Christ Jesus! It's the bridge of faith that takes you from the natural things in life to the supernatural things of God! God bless and much love.

# Daily Devotions

———◈◈◈◈———

Good morning! Read Romans 6:13–18 and 7:15–25. Life is full of difficult challenges. Often the things we intend to say and do, we don't, and the things we wish to avoid we say and do! It must be understood that it's the sin nature that lives within! Therefore, it's extremely necessary to hold tightly to the spiritual nature of the Holy Spirit that also lives within, having a conscious thought of everything you say and do! Remember, it's not you but sin that lives within that's your biggest challenge! God bless and much love.

# Daily Devotions

Good morning! Read Lamentations 3:1–7 and 19–26. Everyone goes through some form of affliction, whether it's our health, financial, relationships, etc. We pray but feel our prayers are unanswered. However, for the child of God, we reflect on and remember the good things God has done! Therefore we have hope! We understand that the mercies of God never fail. If God has allowed us to go through something, He will most surely bring us through whereas a greater blessing is in the end. It's the grace of God that sustains us! God bless and much love.

# Daily Devotions

---

Good morning! Read Jeremiah 50:6 and 1 Peter 3:12. Many of us have that friend or friends who we never hear from until we are needed. Sadly, many believers in Christ are in that same category when it comes to their relationship with God. When God calls, many don't answer or many ignore His calling. God constantly wants to spend time with us, but many give little time to God. But during troubled times, those same individuals expect God to be there. If you want God's time, it's only right that you give Him yours! God bless and much love.

# Daily Devotions

---

Good morning! Read 2 Chronicles 7:14 and Romans 2:4–11. We learn early in life as children that there are consequences for disobedience and rewards for obedience. However, there are many who choose to knowingly do wrong. Being careless and thoughtless in their actions in spite of the consequences. Not understanding that God sees all and hears all and will judge all according to their deeds. What we do will have lasting effects whether good or bad. God's favor is on the obedient, and His wrath awaits the disobedient. God bless and much love.

# Daily Devotions

---

Good morning! Read Isaiah 59:1 and Ephesians 1:17–20. One word or touch from God can change what is to what is not, and what is not to something that is. No other power in heaven or earth can compare to the mighty power of God. If you desire the best, call on the One who can give you what's best. Why settle for worldly power that has an expiration date when the infinite power of God is available to all that seek Him with a pure heart. Believing and obedience with all sincerity draws God's attention. Does He have yours? God bless and much love.

# Daily Devotions

———◇◇◇◇◇———

Good morning! Read Isaiah 40:28–31 and 41:10. There are some days we feel tired and weak but still have to do the things that are necessary for that day. It's during these days (as it should be every day) we must rely on the strength of God to give us the needed strength to do what must be done! God's faithfulness to the faithful is to strengthen them and uphold them with His right hand of righteousness! Are you faithful to God who is faithful to the faithful? Do you draw on His power in your life? God bless and much love.

# Daily Devotions

---

Good morning! Read 2 Chronicles 15:7 and Galatians 6:9, then 2 Timothy 4:5–8. Every long-distance runner trains themselves to run the distance of the course. The run can be exhausting and tiring, but because of their training, they are able to endure. Fighting the good fight of faith is a lifelong fight! It can also be exhausting and tiring at times. When we get exhausted and tired God will breathe new life into us to maintain the good fight! To finish the course and receive our rewards! God bless and much love.

# Daily Devotions

———◇◆◇———

Good morning! Read Mark 11:25–26, then 1 John 4:11–13 and 20–21. God has commanded us to love our neighbor as ourself. Yet there are many who are unforgiving and continue to hold anger and resentment toward others. They profess to love God whom they have not seen but cannot love some of those they see daily. This is not the way nor the will of God. To prove our love for God, we must show God we are forgiving and show love for our neighbor also. Only then is His love perfected in us! God bless and much love.

# Daily Devotions

———◇◆◇◆◇———

Good morning! Read Isaiah 5:20–21 and 2 Corinthians 11:13–15. In today's world with its technology and special effects, the unreal appears to be real. Where fantasy looks like reality so much that for many, the reality is now a fantasy. Sadly for those not rooted in God, God becomes a fantasy as well, leading to false hopes because of this false reality. The reality is that Satan and his angels are able to transform themselves into angels of light to deceive and destroy. Let's not be swayed by the fantasy but hold on to the reality of God in Christ in us. God bless and much love.

# Daily Devotions

———◆✕◆✕◆———

Good morning! Read 2 Chronicles 15:2 and Mark 11: 25–26, then James 4:6–8. What if God gave you as much time as you give Him? What if God forgave you as little as you forgive others? What if God listened to your prayers as much as you listen to Him? What if God drew as close to you as you are willing to be drawn to Him? What if God held back His mercy and grace and plan of salvation to give life to the lifeless and strength to those that are spiritually weak? What if… God bless and much love.

# Daily Devotions

---

Good morning! Read Matthew 6:24 and Luke 9:23–26. There are many who are willing to give their life to Christ but are doing it hesitantly in a halfhearted way. Not willing to give all but wanting to hold on to some things they feel they can't live without. But you cannot serve two masters! You cannot have it your way and completely give your life to Christ! You must lose yourself that you may be found in Him! Willing to take up the cross of Christ daily without shame but having the boldness of Christ living within! God bless and much love.

# Daily Devotions

---

Good morning! Read Matthew 5:10–16. The children of God will face criticism from those who don't know God. Having our faith questioned often in an effort to disprove the truth of our belief. But as God is our light, we are also the light to the world in Christ Jesus. It's by our works that testify of our faith! It's the Light of Christ in us that shines brightly that all may see and witness the anointing that God has put upon us. It's the light in us that glorifies God and His righteousness! God bless and much love.

# Daily Devotions

———◈◈◈◈◈———

G ood morning! Read Genesis 25:1–2 and Job 33:25, then Isaiah 40:28–31. A costly thing anyone can do is underestimate the ability and power of someone else. However, many underestimate the ability and power of God. God's ability and power has not diminished over time. As God did with Abraham, having a child well into his advanced age and having more children past the age of one hundred after the death of Sarah. The strength and power of God working in our life is grounded in our faith in Him! God bless and much love.

# Daily Devotions

———◇◈◇———

Good morning! Read Mark 12:1–11. Jesus often spoke in parables. Showing an earthly illustration with a spiritual meaning. The parable about the vineyard is more than just a parable. It brings to light how God spoke through His prophets and how the prophets were mistreated. It also brings to light God sending His Son and the death of His Son. It also gives clear warning and forecast the anger of God for the treatment of those who uphold His Word and speak in His name. What has been rejected has become the head of the corner. God bless and much love.

# Daily Devotions

---

Good morning! Read Psalm 119:103–105 and 130, then Jeremiah 15:16. Most ideas of what people have about God and Satan are what they see portrayed and depicted in movies or television or someone's idea of who they think they are. No movie or program or opinion is as accurate as the book itself. To know the complete truth, you must read and understand the complete book. Bits and pieces will not give anyone a complete understanding of what anything is. Only by reading the book can you truly know. God bless and much love.

# Daily Devotions

———◇◇◇◇◇◇———

Good morning! Read 2 Chronicles 7:14 and Malachi 3:7. As we grow from childhood to adulthood, there is change in our relationships with those we have known over the years. Many drift away from those of their youth to having new relationships with those they've come to know as they've grown older. Sadly, many also have grown and drifted away from God! However, God is patient and full of mercy and grace and willing to forgive and welcome your return home to Him! It's that time! Come home! God bless and much love.

# Daily Devotions

———◇◇◇———

Good morning! Read Matthew 16:24–26 and Luke 12:16–21. There are many who invest in many things to provide for security for their future. Searching for the best investments that will yield the best return on what they hope will secure a desired future outcome. However, the best investment anyone can make is to invest their life in Christ! It's by losing your life in Christ in this life that you are saving your life for eternal glory with God in the next! Having the treasure of eternal life in God's kingdom is priceless! God bless and much love.

# Daily Devotions

---

Good morning! Read Matthew 13:3–9 and 18–23. There are many who make commitments but lack the staying power to stay with them. To have staying power, you need preparation beforehand that will fuel your commitment. To receive the Word of God also takes preparation to have the staying power to stay with it in spite of the devil's distractions to keep you from it. Prayer and humility and believing are the first steps in preparation needed to have the staying power needed to receive the Word of God! God bless and much love.

# Daily Devotions

———◇◇◇◇◇———

Good morning! Read Philippians 4:5–7 and 1 Peter 5:6–7. Often we make a list, whether a grocery list, a list of our day's activities, a list of things to do, etc. Sadly, some also have a worry list, whether financial worries, health worries, relationship worries, job worries, and so on. The best solution for your worry list is to make it your prayer list. By doing so, you remove it from your hands and put it in God's hands. Only then can the peace of God comfort your heart and mind. When you pray more, you worry less! God bless and much love.

# Daily Devotions

---

Good morning! Read Proverbs 24:16 and 1 Corinthians 9:24–27. There's an old saying, "Winners never quit and quitters never win!" This is true in our pursuit in the race of life! It's the doing of what's good in life that inspires us to keep going despite the obstacles that may confront us. Our good works are inspiring to all who take notice of our good deeds and also gain us favor with God. It's His strength that enables us to keep moving forward. Although we may fall at times, the Spirit of God will refresh us! God bless and much love.

# Daily Devotions

---

Good morning! Read Philippians 4:5–7 and 1 Peter 5:6–7. Often we make a list, whether a grocery list, a list of our days activities, a list of things to do, etc. Sadly, some also have a worry list, whether financial worries, health worries, relationship worries, job worries, and so on. The best solution for your worry list is to make it your prayer list. By doing so you remove it from your hands and put it in God's hands. Only then can the peace of God comfort your heart and mind. When you pray more, you worry less! God bless and much love.

# Daily Devotions

———◇◆◇———

Good morning! Read Lamentations 3:19–26. As we grow older, we look back on our life and take note on how far we've come. From our beginning to where we are today and where we hope to be in the tomorrows to come. For those who have trusted God, we are humbled and thankful that we have not been consumed by the things that have consumed others. Understanding that it's God's mercy and grace and His faithfulness that has brought us this far and will continue to carry us because of His love and compassion for those who love Him. God bless and much love.

# Daily Devotions

———◈◈◈◈◈———

Good morning! Read Romans 12:1–2 and 2 Corinthians 8:11–12, then Colossians 3:5–10. When our trash can is full, we remove the trash bag and replace it with a new bag. We can also replace the trash in our mind with a new mindset. We can remove all fear, doubt, hate, unforgiveness, and any sinful way of thinking and replace it with confidence, forgiveness, love, and self-respect to live a godly and righteous life. But you must be willing to do so. A clean house is more comfortable to live in than one filled with filth. God bless and much love.

# Daily Devotions

---

Good morning! Read Psalm 119:33–35 and 1 Timothy 2:4–6. The best and most accurate information is what we receive firsthand. Getting information from a second or third party is never as complete or as accurate as when we receive it firsthand. We learn more from having the working experience doing anything than being told how something is done. God wants to give us firsthand knowledge and experience that knowledge to gain understanding of Him! God's class is always in session! God bless and much love.

# Daily Devotions

---

Good morning! Read Philippians 4:4–7 and 11–13. When we put our trust in God, we can find joy in every situation no matter how bleak things may look. Knowing it is a growing process we are going through. Just another step to the top of the staircase that leads to the purpose and plan God has for us. Our hearts and minds are given peace as we learn that we can do all things and through Christ Jesus when we believe. To have a balanced life whether things are going good or bad. Rejoicing in the Lord always along the way. God bless and much love.

# Daily Devotions

———◆◆◆———

Good morning! Read Isaiah 26:3–4 and 40:28–31, then Matthew 11:28–30. Every morning, many start their day with a cup of coffee or an energy drink to get their day started. They seek the advice of counselors or friends seeking to find the answer to the burdens they are weighed down by in life. Running in an endless cycle that doesn't seem to end. All the while God is saying, "Look unto Me." True peace and true strength can only be found in the One that gives it to all that call upon Him. Why keep waiting? Make the call! God bless and much love.

# Daily Devotions

———◇◇◇◇◇———

Good morning! Read Matthew 11:28–30 and Philippians 4:5–7. Are you too blessed to be stressed? Or are you too stressed to "feel" blessed? Being stressful can block and shield the blessings of God in your life. Stress creates anxiety, fear and doubt that holds you hostage in your own mind. It's by the grace of God and the love of God that we can lay our burdens and concerns down before Him! By doing so the Peace of God will "keep your heart and mind through Christ Jesus!" Remove the stress to be blessed! God bless and much love.

# Daily Devotions

———✦———

Good morning! Read Matthew 11:28–30 and Philippians 4:5–7. Are you too blessed to be stressed? Or are you too stressed to feel blessed? Being stressful can block and shield the blessings of God in your life. Stress creates anxiety, fear, and doubt that hold you hostage in your own mind. It's by the grace of God and the love of God that we can lay our burdens and concerns down before Him! By doing so the peace of God will keep your heart and mind through Christ Jesus! Remove the stress to be blessed! God bless and much love.

# Daily Devotions

———◇◇◇◇◇———

Good morning! Read Matthew 6:33–34 and Philippians 4:19, then Hebrews 4:16. Whenever we have a need, we turn to those who can help us in our time of need, hoping they have the ability to help us in our time of need where we have lack. Unfortunately, many look to others instead of looking to God first for direction. It's at His throne of grace where we obtain mercy and find grace to help in our time of need. God wants us to come boldly in faith with expectation that God will supply our need as promised. God bless and much love.

# Daily Devotions

———◇◇◇◇———

Good morning! Read 2 Chronicles 15:2 and Zechariah 1:3, then James 4:8. Many times in life we have gone astray. Doing things we know we shouldn't and saying things we know we shouldn't say. This is the time to get your house in order! To get back on the right track that we know we should be on. To recommit to what is good and that goodness is returning to God! If you seek Him, you will find Him. If you return to God, God will return to you. But you must be of single mind to do the will of God! God bless and much love.

# Daily Devotions

---

Good morning! Read Proverbs 16:6–9 and Isaiah 26:3–4. When your ways are pleasing to God what seems to be unlikely becomes likely. What seems to be impossible becomes possible. When your ways are pleasing to God, God causes even your enemies to be at peace with you. When your ways are pleasing to God, you are surrounded by His perfect peace and His favor is continuously with you. We are pleasing to God when our trust, faith, and hope are in Him! Are your ways pleasing to God? God bless and much love.

# Daily Devotions

———◇◇◇◇◇———

Good morning! Read Proverbs 16:1–3 and 9 and Matthew 10:5–8. In team sports, each team prepares a strategy and plan to defeat the opposing team. However, it's the execution of that plan of each individual player that brings success to the team. It's important that each player does their part for the team! Many players playing as one! We, as children of God, are to work as one in our spreading of the gospel of Christ! To preach and teach and share the plan of salvation God has for all who submit their lives to Him. God bless and much love.

# Daily Devotions

---

Good morning! Read Isaiah 26:3–4 and Jeremiah 33:2.3. World peace has eluded our world for hundreds and thousands of years. However, having the peace of God and living in the peace of God has also been available for hundreds and thousands of years! The choice is quite simple: you can look to the world hoping to have peace, or you can keep your mind stayed on God where His perfect peace prevails to all who hunger for His peace and everlasting strength! Finding peace in a world that's still searching for peace! God bless and much love.

# Daily Devotions

———◇◆◇———

Good morning! Read Psalm 12:6 and 1 Thessalonians 5:23–24, then Hebrews 4:12. God is powerful, and there is power in the Word of God! However, for God's Word to benefit you in your life, you must first know and understand His Word. The devil will try to create doubt and influence you to question God's Word just as he did Adam and Eve in the garden of Eden. But God's Word is not to be questioned but to be accepted and believed! To believe the truth of God's Word, you must first accept His Word as truth! God bless and much love.

# Daily Devotions

---

G ood morning! Read Philippians 3:13–15. We all have gone through bad experiences in life. Some to a greater degree than others and some less. However, harboring and holding on to these experiences can affect your present and future life. What has been done has been done! Holding on to the past will not change the past! It's by forgetting those things which are behind and reaching forth unto those things which are before! To move ahead, you must look ahead to God who knows what lies ahead! God bless and much love.

# Daily Devotions

---

Good morning! Read 2 Corinthians 5:10 and James 4:17. We are rewarded for our obedience. Often it's the relief and satisfaction knowing we have been obedient in doing what we know is the right thing to do. We also know that disobedience has consequences that come from our disobedience. However, knowing to do what is good and right and not doing it is disobedience and a sin in the eyes of God! We are judged according to what we do and don't do as well as what we should do and don't do! God bless and much love.

# Daily Devotions

---

Good morning! Read Romans 5:1–5. To get from point A to point B is followed by a progression of steps that must be done. Without the necessary steps, you will never get from A to B. There are also steps in our getting closer to God. Being justified by faith, we have peace with God through our Lord Jesus Christ. Our step of faith brings us through our tribulations that teaches us patience. Our patience leads us through experience which gives us hope. A hope and assurance of the love of God that is shed into our hearts! God bless and much love.

# Daily Devotions

---◇◇◇◇◇---

Good morning! Read Psalm 37:37–40 and Proverbs 13:20. Often what we hear and see helps shape our viewpoint on what we believe. It's so important that we attune to what is wholesome and right so our viewpoint and what we become to believe is also wholesome and right. Having a good role model or mentor that has earned your trust and respect is often what is needed to keep you on the right path. To become wise, you must associate yourself with those who are wise! A fool runs with other fools! God bless and much love.

# Daily Devotions

---

Good morning! Read 1 John 4:17–21. The greatest feeling that anyone can have is the feeling of being loved. To feel love and to express love to one another is the embodiment of who God is! God is love, and it's His desire that His love is perfected in us. It's the perfected love of God living in us that will cast out all fear and doubt and hate and resentment and anger that you may feel. Replace these negatives with the positives that are found in having godly love that only comes from God who is love! God bless and much love.

# Daily Devotions

---◇◈◇◈◇---

G ood morning! Read Psalm 27:14 and Hebrews 11:6. God is ready and willing to bless all who are ready and willing to receive His blessings. However, many block their blessings by not having the patience to wait on God. Many blessings are also blocked by living a life contrary to the ways of God. Blessings can be blocked by a lack of faith and trust in God. Without faith and trust in God, their hope is weakened. Without hope, there is no faith and trust needed to receive what God is willing to give! God bless and much love.

# Daily Devotions

G ood morning! Read Jude verses 20–25. We face some type of temptation daily. Often we rely on our strength to think what's right, to do what's right, and to live right the best we know how. However, many fall to temptation because of weakness and go through living in regret. But those who live in the love of God maintain their strength and are kept from falling. Because of God's forgiveness, His mercy and grace we are presented faultless before His presence when God is the center of our life! God bless and much love.

# Daily Devotions

---

Good morning! Read Romans 4:20–22 and 8:24–25, then Hebrews:11:1 and 6. We all have hopes and dreams. Hoping and praying for our children's future to be successful. Hoping and praying for our well-being in health and prosperity. Hoping for things we cannot see but having faith in God's direction. Understanding that faith and hope work hand in hand. The two cannot exist without the other. It's our faith and hope in God that pleases God. God in turn rewards our faith when we diligently seek Him. As Abraham staggered not at the promise of God, neither should we. God bless and much love.

# Daily Devotions

---

Good morning! Read 2 Chronicles 25:9 and Joel 2:25–28, then 2 Corinthians 5:17. Many indulge in things they should not and overindulge in others. Whether it's spending, eating, drinking, or doing drugs, a measure of guilt follows. Putting themselves in a hole that seems impossible to recover from. Looking to find ways to recover from the setback they're now in. God has promised to restore and recover that which is lost to make all things new. Put aside looking back and look to God for a new beginning. God bless and much love.

# Daily Devotions

---

ood morning! Read Ezekiel 36:24–28 and 2 Corinthians 5:17–21. There are some things in everyone's life where they wish they can have a do-over. To change or wash away what has been done. To forget some things of the past and start anew. This is a small challenge for Almighty God! God can change the unchangeable and make the crooked paths straight! But you must allow Him to cleanse you of who you've become that you can be the best you can be! Believe and be reconciled to God! God bless and much love.

# Daily Devotions

---

G ood morning! Read Psalm 121:1–5 and Philippians 4:19. When we have needs, we go to great lengths and exhaust every avenue to have those needs met. But many still fall short of what's needed to fulfill their needs. However, those who put their trust in God to fulfill their needs will lift up their eyes unto the hills for their help! Knowing and firmly believing that God, who is always with us, will supply all their needs according to His riches in Christ Jesus! If you call upon God, He will answer! Have you made the call? God bless and much love.

# Daily Devotions

---

Good morning! Read John 16:13–14 and 2 Corinthians 4:13–18. From the day we are born, we go through an aging process. We grow up to a point, and then our physical being slowly declines over time. However, when we are born again by the Spirit of God, we are renewed daily in growth by His Spirit within us. It does not decline over time but is continuously filled and overflowing. Teaching us and guiding us every day of our lives. It is the fountain of youth to our spirit and soul! Never ending but eternal! God bless and much love.

# Daily Devotions

———◇◈◇———

Good morning! Read Psalm 51:10 and 119:105, then Proverbs 4:23. Whenever you bake a cake, you must follow the instructions in the recipe. All the ingredients down to the temperature must be followed. Following the wrong instructions will bring wrong results. But following the right instructions brings the right results. God's Word is the recipe for life. Following the instructions will bring right results. You cannot wash dirty dishes with dirty water and expect them to be clean. God's Word will cleanse and change your life if you follow the instructions! God bless and much love.

# Daily Devotions

———◇◇◇◇◇———

Good morning! Read Galatians 5:22–25. There are many spirits in heaven and the world that influence and direct the lives of everyone. Being influenced and directed by the spirits of the world is like eating bad or rotten fruit. It may be sweet to the taste, but it becomes bitter to the body and soul, ruining the lives of all who taste. However, the fruit of the Holy Spirit of God brings health to all that seek him. It is sweet to our spiritual taste and rewards our spiritual body as it grows. Taste and see that the Lord is good! God bless and much love.

# Daily Devotions

---

Good morning! Read John 4:10–14 and 6:47–51, then Romans 8:26–28. There are times we want to pray and need to pray but can't find the words we want to express to God in prayer. It's during these times that the Holy Spirit makes intercession on our behalf with what's in our heart and mind to God. It's also the Holy Spirit that quenches our spiritual thirst from the fountain of living waters and feeds our spiritual hunger with the bread of life! All working together for the good because of our love for God! God bless and much love.

# Daily Devotions

———◇◇◇◇◇———

Good morning! Read Psalm 122:1 and Hebrews 10:24–25. We always get excited for family get-togethers and gatherings with our friends. Always with anticipation of the good time we know we're going to have. To catch up on what's happening in their lives and them catching up on what's happening in our life. It's God's desire that we have this same excitement and anticipation when we gather together in His name! To enter His house with joy and to uplift one another in the name of Christ Jesus! God bless and much love.

# Daily Devotions

———◇◇◇◇◇———

Good morning! Read 2 Samuel 22:3–7 and 29–33. Whenever we need something done, we go to someone we know will get it done. Whenever we need protection or help, we go to someone we know we can count on. We are grateful for their help and for always being there. They have earned our trust by their loyalty to us over time. Our God is there in times of distress and hears our cry. We show our gratitude by glorifying God in our giving of thanks for all that He's done. We praise Him because He is worthy to be praised! God bless and much love.

# Daily Devotions

———◈◈◈◈◈———

Good morning! Read Proverbs 4:23 and 6:16–23. There are things we do that are right or wrong in our eyes. Much of what we do or don't do is based on our character. God looks at who we are from the heart—how we look, what we say, what we imagine in our heart, and how we treat others. The things of the heart are what matters most to God. God hates an evil and scheming heart more than our actions. His Word is a light and lamp to reprove and instruct us in the ways of life to be pleasing in His sight. To do good, you have to be good! God bless and much love.

# Daily Devotions

---

Good morning! Read Isaiah 1:16–20 and 5:25, then 43:1–2. Many children of God are like a sinking boat, taking in water and trying to row without removing the water that's filling the boat. So too are our sins in the eyes of God. God has stretched forth His hand of mercy to forgive and His grace to remove what's causing our lives to sink. To lift us high above the stormy seas of life, we often struggle through trying to get to the other side. To the land where we can find rest. Reach for and grab hold of God's helping hand! God bless and much love.

# Daily Devotions

———✦◇✦———

Good morning! Read Proverbs 4:20–27. Every day we have the opportunity to turn the page and start a new chapter in life. How the chapter goes is dependent on the choices we make. The wise will make wise choices and decisions to enhance their life and the lives of those around them. Each choice and decision is heartfelt in the sincerity of truth! Understanding that the heart holds the issues of life! Those who are wise must be wise in heart! Begin your new chapter in life today! Why wait? God bless and much love.

# Daily Devotions

---

Good morning! Read Isaiah 26:3–4 and 49:16. We are relieved when our assurances and our hopes and dreams have become certainties. When we are absolutely sure that the results are final! For the child of God, this absolute certainty is knowing that our lives have been written in the palm of the hands of God! That we are always in His mind, and our ways are always before Him! Knowing this gives us absolute certainty so we can live in perfect peace when we keep our minds stayed on Him! God bless and much love.

# Daily Devotions

———◈◈◈◈◈———

G ood morning! Read Joel 2:25–27 and 2 Corinthians 5:17–18. When something is broken or damaged and needs repair, we go to someone who is skilled in repairing that which needs repair. Even after it's repaired, it never is as good as it was originally. Many have lives that are broken and damaged and need repair. Only God, who is our Maker and Creator, is skilled enough to repair the lives of those who are broken and damaged. When God restores and repairs, your life is better than new! God bless and much love.

# Daily Devotions

———◇◇◇◇◇———

Good morning! Read Ephesians 2:4–10. In the game of baseball, there is a starting pitcher, a middle relief pitcher, and a closer to finish the game when the game is on the line. We begin life as that starting pitcher. Giving our all and doing our best to win this game of life. But there comes a time in life when we tire and need help. We call on God who sends His Holy Spirit, who is our relief pitcher, to sustain us in this game of life. Finally, it is the grace of God (our closer) who causes us to triumph in this game of life! God bless and much love.

# Daily Devotions

---

Good morning! Read Matthew 7:7–12 and 11:28–30. If there is something you need or want and don't ask for it, the answer is the same as no. If there is something you need to seek and don't look, it will never be found. To get the attention of someone on the other side of a door, you have to knock. If you don't knock, the door won't be answered. God is waiting for us to come to Him and ask of Him what we desire. To seek Him in all we do. To open the door we desire to enter. Just ask, seek, and knock! God bless and much love.

# Daily Devotions

———◈※◈———

Good morning! Read Psalm 42:11 and 119:11, then Isaiah 29:10–16 and Galatians 6:7–10. How can anyone walk with God and be obedient to God when they have closed themselves off to the Word of God? Talking among themselves or hearing someone else speak the words of God and not know the Word of God for themselves. Or making an occasional appearance to the house of God, but their heart is far removed from the teachings of God. If this is you, it's time to rededicate and recommit! God bless and much love.

# Daily Devotions

---

Good morning! Read Galatians 5:16–25. Every day we are moved in many directions to do things. We are moved by certain thoughts and feelings in the decisions we make. We are also moved by the desires of the flesh that is contrary to the things and thoughts of the spirit. There is a constant inward battle between the flesh and the spirit. The one you feed will become the stronger! Overcome the flesh by feeding your spirit! If you feed the spirit, you will be led by the spirit! Be strong and be moved by the spirit! God bless and much love.

# Daily Devotions

Good morning! Read John 15:1–11. To be born again by the Spirit of God, we become a new creation in Christ. The seed of His Spirit is planted within us, and we are now planted in the garden of God. Our lives become nourished and watered by His Spirit so our lives can grow and bear much fruit. Without God's continuous nourishment, we cannot grow! Without the continuous watering of His Word in our lives, the fruit that we bear is not sweetened! Is your life being nourished and watered by God? God bless and much love.

# Daily Devotions

———◇◈◇———

Good morning! Read John 15:16. There is always great joy when we feel and know we are accepted by our peers. To have their support and encouragement is helpful in our daily walk in life. We are appreciative and don't want to let them down but strive to show them we are worthy of their friendship. We are also chosen and loved by God! God also encourages us and supports us in our daily walk in life. Let's also show our appreciation and strive to prove to our peers we are worthy being His child! God bless and much love.

# Daily Devotions

---

Good morning! Read Psalm 104:1–5 and 10–14, then Isaiah 26:3–4. God has blessed His children and we, His children, bless God in the giving of thanks for all He has done. God has created everything in perfect order. The stars in the heavens to the rivers and streams and mountains. From the smallest form of life to the greatest. God has created all in perfect order. Our imperfections can be perfected when we allow God to bring His perfect order into our life. To know His perfect peace by keeping our mind on Him. God bless and much love.

# Daily Devotions

———◈◈◈———

Good morning! Read Psalm 40:1–8 and Hebrews 11:6. Being a child of God requires patience. A willingness to be steadfast and trust God in all circumstances. To open up your heart in prayer because He hears our prayers. God will put a new song in our heart and a new outlook on life itself. God is faithful to the faithful and a strong refuge to those that seek Him. Without faith, you cannot please God. You must believe that He is and strive to do His will. To know God's will is to know God's word. God bless and much love.

# Daily Devotions

Good morning! Read Matthew 6:19–21 and Luke 12:16–21. There are many on a quest to accumulate material things—nice clothes, cars, a nice home, financial abundance, etc. There is nothing wrong with having nice things as long as they don't have you! However, nothing in the material world can you take with you into the afterlife. It's only the spiritual treasures of your riches toward God that can be carried into the afterlife of eternity! Is your heart on material things or spiritual treasures toward God? God bless and much love.

# Daily Devotions

---✦---

Good morning! Read Psalm 139:7–14 and Isaiah 9:16–17. Everything you say and do is always in the presence of God. Every heartbeat and every breath you take is in God's presence. Whether you believe in God or not, you are in the presence of God! Many who believe and many who wear the cloak of sin are still in the presence of God! Because of God's mercy and grace and His willingness to forgive, His anger is not turned away, but His hand is stretched out still! You are always in His presence! God bless and much love.

# Daily Devotions

---

Good morning! Read Joshua 24:15. and Jeremiah 29:11–13. The Israelites crossed over the Red Sea and were freed from the oppression of Pharaoh. The Israelites also crossed the Jordan River to reach the promise land. God made it possible by parting both the Red Sea and the Jordan River. Only by crossing over was it possible for a change for the better to happen. By crossing over from our old ways to God do we find our promise land that God has planned for us. Have you crossed over? God bless and much love.

# Daily Devotions

———◇❉❉◇———

Good morning! Read Galatians 1:10 and 2 Timothy 2:15. There are many who seek to be accepted and approved by their peers, going to great lengths in giving of their time, finances, etc., to win the acceptance and approval of their peers they feel they need. However, it's the approval of God that matters most! It's the giving of your time to God and studying His Word that meets God's approval. Whose approval matters most to you? That of your peers who cannot save your soul or the approval of God who can? God bless and much love.

# Daily Devotions

———⬦⬦⬦———

ood morning! Read 1 Corinthians 12:4–14. God has given each one of us certain natural skills and abilities. But it's up to us to master the skills and abilities God has given. God has also made available spiritual gifts to complement and enhance the natural skills and abilities we have. It must be understood that all gifts, both natural and spiritual, are to complement one another, and we are to work together in a complementary fashion that will enhance the lives of one another that we may live as one in Christ! God bless and much love.

# Daily Devotions

---

Good morning! Read Romans 10:17 and 1 Timothy 2:1–6. There are many that don't read the Bible because they have a hard time understanding it. This is a stumbling block the devil puts in the path of those who have a desire to learn of God. Limiting and/or destroying their hope and faith that is found in the Bible. Unable to experience the truth of God and gain understanding through that experience. The devil puts a wedge between us and God, but Christ is the meditator that keeps us one with God! God bless and much love.

# Daily Devotions

———◇◆◇———

Good morning! Read Isaiah 45:23 and 2 Corinthians 5:10, then Philippians 2:10–11. There are many who refuse to give God the respect and honor He deserves. Being swayed through unbelief and being skeptical about the existence of God. Having a form of belief that suits them and willfully ignoring the Word of God. Seeing God at a distance if at all. Not realizing that our time in this life is short in comparison to eternity. What is certain is that all will one day die. All will be judged, and every knee *will* bow before God. No exceptions! God bless and much love.

# Daily Devotions

---

Good morning! Read Luke 5:36–38. When we get a new set of clothes we always get washed up and cleaned up before we put them on to wear. We don't put new clothes on a dirty body if we want to look our best. So too if we want to live unto God. We must remove our old self to put on the newness of Christ. We need to be cleaned and washed in His blood that we may put on this new righteousness found in God through Him. The old is not compatible with the new. Either choose the new or live in the old. God bless and much love.

# Daily Devotions

———◇◇◇———

Good morning! Read Isaiah 55:6–13. Often many go through life looking and seeking answers and directions to take in life. They have their thoughts and ways about doing things. But it's the seeking of God that answers many of the questions and provides the directions needed when your trust is placed in His hands! God's thoughts and ways are far above our understanding. God sees what's around the corner of life whereas we can't! God sees the tomorrows we have yet to live! Seek Him, He knows! God bless and much love.

# Daily Devotions

---

Good morning! Read Matthew 6:5–13 and James 5:16. Prayer for the child of God is essential and important. Our prayers should not be repetitive or merely words without meaning but should be moving and felt in the heart. If our prayers are not moving and felt in the heart, we cannot expect our prayers to be moving and felt in the heart of God! It's through our prayers that our faith is increased and our hope and trust in God is confirmed. Our prayers should be heartfelt and sincere to God! God bless and much love.

# Daily Devotions

———◇◇◇◇◇———

Good morning! Read Psalm 91:1–6 and 9–12. When it rains, we use an umbrella. During the sunny hot days of summer, many use an umbrella to block the hot sunlight or some type of sunblock to keep from getting sunburned. They are a shield to protect us. When we abide under the shadow of the Almighty, we are protected from what could harm us. The secret place of God is our umbrella and sunblock to protect us when we find shelter in Him. He is our covering! The truth of God is our shield! God bless and much love.

# Daily Devotions

———◈◇◈———

Good morning! Read Ecclesiastes 3:1–8 and Acts 17:29–31, then Ephesians 1:4–7. There is a reason for everything that happens, has happened, and will happen. Even the time of day and minute we are born has already been recorded in the mind of God. God saw who would receive Him and who would reject Him before we came into being. Just as God has set the seasons in motion from winter to fall, our life is also in motion from our birth to our earthly departure. There is a time for all seasons, and this is the season of repentance. God bless and much love.

# Daily Devotions

---

Good morning! Read Mark 9:21–24 and 11:22–24, then John 14:12–15. Jesus declared that if we believed in Him, we would not only have eternal life, but we also would be able to do the things He did. This comes from having faith and believing in the power of God behind it. Demonstrating through us the power of God working in our lives. Believing in God and the power of His might is the first step. Jesus is not speaking to someone else but is speaking to you and me to believe on Him whom God has sent. God bless and much love.

# Daily Devotions

———◇❈◇———

Good morning! Read Jeremiah 9:23–24. There are many who are satisfied and proud of their accomplishments. Some with their intellectual academic accomplishments, others with their self-proclaimed wisdom and still others with their materialistic wealth. All finding glory and glorifying themselves at their resume in life! However, those who know God are humble in their accomplishments and are thankful to God and find their greatest glory in knowing and understanding Him! God bless and much love.

# Daily Devotions

———✦———

G ood morning! Read Proverbs 18:21 and Ephesians 4:29, then James 3:5–10. Every day many nations are on a quest to develop more powerful and destructive weapons. But the most powerful weapon is that of the tongue with the words we speak. It's the spoken word of God that brought everything into existence. It's also the spoken word by us that can edify the life of someone or bring them emotional harm. God's Word is life, and when our conversation is based on His Word, it brings life to the hearer! God bless and much love.

# Daily Devotions

———◇◇◇◇◇———

G ood morning! Read Isaiah 40:28–31 and Zechariah 4:5–6. There is so much strength and power in each of us. However, it is the power of the Spirit of God that gives us strength to have the power that we do have. We can condition our bodies to keep ourselves in great physical shape, but we first must have the mindset to do so. When we have a godly connection to God, we will surpass our expectations. Remember, it's not our power or our strength, but it's the Spirit of God working within us! God bless and much love.

# Daily Devotions

---◇◇◇◇◇---

Good morning! Read Luke 17:11–19. Much of the world is seeking God less and putting their trust in themselves rather than acknowledging God. That is until there's a crisis that cannot be controlled. Sadly, God gets the blame for the tragedy. What's even sadder is the tragedy could maybe have been avoided if God were accepted more in the lives of the people. Only during a crisis are heads turned back to God for deliverance. When delivered, then heads sadly turn away again. Praise and thank God without ceasing daily! God bless and much love.

# Daily Devotions

———◇◆◇———

Good morning! Read 1 Kings 19:11–12 and Psalm 46:10, then John 16:12–15 and Hebrews 1:1–3 To hear the voice of God, you must be filled with the Spirit of God and have a heart for God and what the Spirit is saying. Hearing from God then speaking His word into your life to change and enhance your life to carry you through the changes that occur in your life. God has given us His word that confirms His voice. But we must be still and listen to what the voice of the Spirit of God is saying. God bless and much love.

# Daily Devotions

———◇◈◇———

Good morning! Read Psalm 19:14 and Proverbs 3:5–6. The "prayer of faith" is so important in the life of those who believe in God. It's through our humility and sincerity that our prayers are accepted by God. Our prayer of faith is trusting in God and asking God to strengthen us in Him that we lean not unto our own understanding but to acknowledge Him in all our ways and to seek His direction every day of our life. Understanding and knowing God is our Lord, our strength, and our Redeemer! God bless and much love.

# Daily Devotions

———◇◈◇◈◇———

G ood morning! Read Ezekiel 36:25–28. There is constant development in the things we use—faster cars, improved high-tech equipment such as cell phones and televisions, new and better ways to prepare our food, etc. However, the most important improvement that we all need is a new and improved heart. Only God can remove the callous, hateful, and uncaring heart that many have and replace it with a heart that improves your life. A heart that yearns for God and appreciates the love God has for you! God bless and much love.

# Daily Devotions

———◆◇◆◇◆———

Good morning! Read Matthew 6:24–34. There are many who work hard and are living from paycheck to paycheck! Never feeling they make enough or have enough to make ends meet! This can cause frustration, anxiety, and stress, building worry on top of worry! But God says, "Don't worry!" If God can take care of the birds in the air, the fish in the sea, and everything He has created, He most assuredly will take care of us! The key is to seek Him first! To have complete faith knowing God will make a way! God bless and much love.

# Daily Devotions

Good morning! Read 1 Chronicles 14:14–17 and 2 Chronicles 20:15, then 2 Corinthians 12:7–10 and Philippians 4:13. God allows His children to go through a measure of trials as we grow in faith in Him. With each trial, we witness the demonstration of the power of God as we are strengthened during times of weakness. By seeking God's direction and allowing God to work in our life, we know that with each challenge and trial we face, God is already there. Making a way for us knowing that the victory is ours because of Him. God bless and much love.

# Daily Devotions

---

G ood morning! Read James 1:2–8 and 4:1–3. Answered prayers are joyful. It's having patience for prayers to be answered that's hard. This is an exercise in endurance of our heart and mind in building of our trust and faith. It's not giving up but enduring to the end that we receive the bountiful blessings of God. God's timing is perfect timing. He is never late but answers our prayers in due season. Being obedient and not lustful are key to answered prayer. It's not through pride but with humility that we call upon God in prayer. God bless and much love.

# Daily Devotions

---

Good morning! Read Luke 10:16 and John 16:13–15. When the Spirit of God lives within you, there is a yearning to speak the things of the Spirit. At times your words are rejected by others, thinking they're your words and not understanding it's the Spirit of God speaking through you. Understand that if they are rejecting you, they are also rejecting Christ who lives within you! However, His Word must be spoken faithfully, sincerely, and truthfully! But to speak His Word in this manner, you must know His Word! Do you? God bless and much love.

# Daily Devotions

---

G ood morning! Read 1 Corinthians 13:1–13. It's the love, mercy, and grace of God that sustains us. God's example to us is that we have this same love, mercy, and grace toward one another. If we attain great understanding in many things or do many meaningful deeds and not have the love, mercy, and grace toward one another, it is meaningless in the eyes of God. If we are not forgiving and lack the love needed, we really are not following the example of God! It's love, mercy, and grace that counts! God bless and much love.

# Daily Devotions

———⟨⟩———

Good morning! Read 2 Kings 19:32–35 and 2 Chronicles 20:15–17. God has always fought for and defended His children when they have been threatened or attacked. Just as we are protective of our children, so is God protective of His. As God was then, so is He now to those who call on His Name for deliverance. Only let's not forget or take what God has done for granted! He is there when we need Him and when we feel we don't. It's because of His great love for us! We are never alone! God is always there! God bless and much love.

# Daily Devotions

---

Good morning! Read Psalm 51:1–12 and John 8:31–32, then 2 Timothy 1:7. We often pray to be delivered and to be free. However, our biggest burden can be ourselves. Our selfishness and greed and not letting go of who we are to become who God would have us to be. Being in bondage to ourselves and holding ourselves back from the freedom found only in Christ Jesus. It is not how we see the truth but how the truth is in God when we learn and know His truth. We are born into sin, but to be born again in Christ, we find the freedom we desire. God bless and much love.

# Daily Devotions

---

Good morning! Read Isaiah 40:3–8 and 2 Corinthians 7:1, then 1 Thessalonians 4:16–18. Those that don't know God and Christ can see their righteousness in us when we live and walk in the ways and live in the promises of God. We don't grow into righteousness but are righteous as we grow in Christ Jesus. We are the voice of the one crying in the wilderness, proclaiming God and the return one day of His son Jesus Christ. Let nothing be said or done to tarnish your standing in Christ. God bless and much love.

# Daily Devotions

———◇◇◇◇◇◇———

G ood morning! Read Romans 4:19–21 and Hebrews chapter 11 and James 2:26. The more we do something, the better we get at doing it. This is also true when it comes to living out our faith! The more we exercise our faith, the stronger we become in faith! Our problems are overshadowed by our faith in the promises of God. By living out our faith, we are also a living example to the faithless and give hope to the hopeless. The eleventh chapter of Hebrews is a great example of living out our faith! God bless and much love.

# Daily Devotions

———◇◆◇———

Good morning! Read Job 23:6–14 and Psalm 27:1, then Matthew 6:33–34. We cannot see the wind, but we know it's there because we feel it. We cannot see God, but we know He's there because by His mercy and grace we are here. The evidence is seen and felt in our lives by our confidence and faith in God's working in our life. The strength God gives us when we are weak and how He lights the path of life for all who believe. God is the light and salvation of our life. He is the strength of our life that we need not be afraid. God bless and much love.

# Daily Devotions

---

Good morning! Read Luke 9:23–26, then Galatians 1:10 and 2:20. Whom do you seek to persuade and impress? Is it your family and friends who cannot give you salvation but will surely die one day as you? Or is it God who can give salvation and eternal life to all that believe in His words of life? To impress others, we say, do, and give things that are temporary and will one day fade away. God requires us to crucify ourselves and give our lives to Him that Christ may live in us. This is eternal life found only in Christ Jesus. God bless and much love.

# Daily Devotions

———❖❖❖———

Good morning! Read 2 Peter 1:20–21. There are many who reject the Bible believing it was written by men and not God. Yet they believe newspapers, magazines, social media, etc., that is definitely written by men and women! The writers of the Bible were moved by the Holy Spirit of God to write what has been written, similar to a manager dictating a letter to a secretary. The secretary does the writing, but the words are those of the manager. The Bible is God's message to His children who believe! God bless and much love.

# Daily Devotions

———◇◈◇———

G ood morning! Read Judges 7:2 and 1 Samuel 17:45, then John 17:16–17. The children of God are independent of the world but dependent on God. Being separated from the world and sanctified by the Word of God to live unto God. Not glorifying ourselves but giving all glory to God! Understanding that it's the power of God that leads us and gives us confidence to face all odds and challenges that come our way. It's His power and strength working in us each day! God bless and much love.

# Daily Devotions

G ood morning! Read 2 Corinthians 4:5–10. Those that strive to do good and live right are the envy of many who lack the inner drive and commitment to do what's right. Looking for faults and criticizing the accomplishments of those who give their all to be the best they can be. The children of God face this negativity in their pursuit to living a life in Christ. Although others may cast us down, we are lifted above this muck and mire and our love and Light of Christ is revealed in us to His glory! God bless and much love.

# Daily Devotions

———◇◇◇◇———

Good morning! Read Romans 8:31 and 1 Corinthians 15:57–58, then Ephesians 6:10–17. There is a saying used in boxing: "Kill the body and the head will die." We are the Body of Christ and Christ is the Head. The devil seeks to kill the body, which is the church, in a vain attempt to defeat the believers in Christ. The devil's only victory is when we fail to realize that our victory is in Christ Jesus. By overcoming fear with faith and the complete armor of God we can stand victorious in every situation the devil attempts to put us through. God bless and much love.

# Daily Devotions

―――――◇◇◇◇◇◇―――――

Good morning! Read Matthew 21:18–22 and Luke 18:27, then Hebrews 11:1. What does it mean to have faith in God? It's having confidence in the power of God to believe the unbelievable knowing that God can make the impossible possible. The devil may put doubt in your mind but don't allow doubt to enter your heart. Doubt will alter and diminish your faith in what God can do. Believing is the active ingredient! God cannot work in you and through you unless you believe. Set your mind and heart to believe God! God bless and much love.

# Daily Devotions

―――――◇◈◇―――――

Good morning! Read Mark 16:15–20 and Romans 10:9–13. When a decision is made to believe and become a follower of Christ, things begin to happen. You are saved through the spiritual baptism of the heart and your eyes are opened to the things of God. It's a feeling you want to share with others and shout to the world! It's a feeling you feel within that cries to come out! It's a feeling of freedom in Christ! This experience is available to all who humble themselves and call upon the name of the Lord to be saved! God bless and much love.

# Daily Devotions

———◆◆◆———

Good morning! Read Romans 10:17. Before a game, every team receives some sort of pep talk. To give the players confidence to play at the best of their ability. To instill in them that the victory is theirs if they believe and have faith in their ability to win. The Word of God gives the pep talk for the Christian! It's by reading and hearing God's Word that we have the confidence to be victorious in our daily life. It's by God's Word and through God's Word that our faith has continuous and unlimited growth! God bless and much love.

# Daily Devotions

───────◇◇◇◇◇───────

Good morning! Read Matthew 5:14–16. The darker the night, the brighter the stars shine. As this world becomes darker because of sin and ungodly acts and unbelief, we, as the children of the Light of God, must shine forth so those living in this darkened world may see hope in God through us. That our light may lead them to His light that they may be saved. That others may flee the coldness that darkness brings to the warmth that light brings. That light is the warmth found through Christ Jesus! God bless and much love.

# Daily Devotions

———◇◈◇———

Good morning! Read Psalm 8:1–9. How often do you give thanks for the simple things in life? Things we seemingly take for granted? The life we have? Our family and friends and loved ones? Those that have come and gone in our life? The victories and blessings God has given us in leading us to where we are this day? As we consider all God has done, we can take heart that God is not finished with us yet. Whatever downfalls we have faced or are facing there is a purpose in it all, that we may see that God is all and in all. But we must consider all and turn to Him! God bless and much love.

# Daily Devotions

---

Good morning! Read Psalm 18:1–6 and 2 Corinthians 10:4. When you're standing on top of the highest mountain, you can see everything for miles. When you're in the valley, all you see is valley. When the rains come, it runs down the sides of the mountain. When rains come in the valley, everything is flooded. God is the rock on top of the mountain. The world is the valley which is overcome with the rain that floods our life. Seek to climb the mountain that is higher than high. To the rock that cannot be moved. God bless and much love.

# Daily Devotions

---

G ood morning! Read Ephesians 6:10–18. That way we dress is normally dependent on the weather or a planned event. From the weather to a social function, we dress accordingly. It's also important that we are dressed spiritually as we face our spiritual battles from day to day. The battles of temptation and fear and all things that may hinder your walk on your path of life! But if you are properly suited in the armor of God, you can withstand and resist all that tries to separate you from your pursuit of God! God bless and much love.

# Daily Devotions

---

Good morning! Read Psalm 23:1–6. The twenty-third Psalm is a song by King David that shows the mercy and grace of God and gives assurance of God's presence in every and all situations. It's a showing of confidence and faith in the darkest of times and the comfort God gives during these times. It's also a promise by God that surely goodness and mercy shall follow us all the days of our life! However, it begins with your trust and faith and believing in the mercy and grace God provides to all who look to Him! God bless and much love.

# Daily Devotions

---

Good morning! Read Matthew 4:4 and 2 Timothy 2:15. As children, our parents often insisted on us eating everything on our plate. Especially the vegetables because of the health benefits they offer. Many Christians give tithes and offerings and take part in worship services and doing things expected of their faith. However, like a child, they shy away from eating their vegetables, which is reading and studying the Word of God! God's Word contains the benefits needed to live a godly life! Eat your veggies! God bless and much love.

# Daily Devotions

———◆◇◆◇◆———

Good morning! Read Ezekiel 36:25–28. There are times when our clothes are stained, and we must get the right stain remover to remove the stain. Like those stained clothes, our hearts are stained by sin, and we need a savior to remove the stain of sin that has engraved itself in our hearts. God can do more than remove the stain of sin in our hearts by giving us a new heart! A new heart with a new spirit that we may begin living a new life! Jesus Christ is our stain remover and Savior to cleanse us to begin again! God bless and much love.

# Daily Devotions

———◇◇◇◇◇———

G ood morning! Read John 16:13–15. We teach what we've been taught. We can't teach what we haven't been taught! If you've been wrongly taught, what you teach will also be wrong. However, if you've been rightly taught, you will rightly teach the right things! The Holy Spirit teaches us the right things of God so we may rightly learn and rightly teach what is right in the eyes of God! Only the Holy Spirit of God can guide you into the truth of God! To rightly teach us so we can teach others! Class is always in session! God bless and much love.

# Daily Devotions

Good morning! Read Matthew 5:14–16 and 2 Corinthians 5:18–21. Our politicians are elected for the people and by the people. They are to represent the people and not themselves! Those called by God are representatives of God and ambassadors for Christ! To represent and reflect the Light of Christ to all living in darkness and searching for light to guide them in a darkened world. We are the light of the world and representatives of the Light that shines in us and through us! Shine brightly that all may see! God bless and much love.

# Daily Devotions

---

Good morning! Read Luke 4:18–19 and John 8:31–32 and 36. Jesus came to set the captives free! Freedom from the bondage of the ungodliness of the ways of the world. We are freed by knowing the Word of God and the Gospel of Christ! When you realize and understand this truth, you must make a conscious effort to live in this truth! Knowing the Word of God and the Gospel of Christ can make you free. However, it's living in the Word of God and the gospel of Christ that keeps you free! Are you free? God bless and much love.

# Daily Devotions

———————◇◇◇◇◇———————

Good morning! Read 2 Chronicles 7:13–14 and Isaiah 9:17, then 1 Timothy 2:4. We serve a loving God who wants to save all. A God of second chances and more to save all from a wicked lifestyle that separates them from God. His hand is steadily reaching out to save the lost. To forgive and heal when they humble themselves in His presence. There is no sin to great that God will not forgive. There is no one to low that cannot be raised. God is ready and willing to light the way for all living in the dark. His hand is stretched out still! God bless and much love.

# Daily Devotions

---

Good morning! Read 1 Thessalonians 4:14–18. We look forward with expectation and anticipation to upcoming holidays. From New Year's through Christmas, we make plans to celebrate these holidays. However, how often do you look with expectation and anticipation for the return of Christ? When Christ returns for His Church with the trump of God! We comfort one another with this expectation and anticipation! To receive His eternal rewards at His coming! Are you prepared? God bless and much love.

# Daily Devotions

---

Good morning! Read Romans 10:9–13 and Ephesians 2:8–10, then Philippians 2:12–13. The salvation of God comes with accepting and receiving Jesus Christ as your personal Savior! Being saved by the grace of God through our faith in Jesus Christ, we don't have to work for our salvation. It is the gift of God! Because it is a gift, we are able to work out our salvation and through our salvation with the Spirit of God working within us! To do God's will and to do the pleasures of God! The grace of God is a priceless gift! God bless and much love.

# Daily Devotions

———⬧⬧⬧———

Good morning! Read 1 Peter 3:10–17. Living your life in the love of God shows appreciation for the life God has given you. To refuse that which is evil and reaching forth to the peace of God available to all who sanctify the Lord God in their hearts. Knowing God's ears are open unto their prayers, but His face is against those who do evil! Having a readiness to answer all who question our reasoning for what we do and why we do it! Understanding it's far better doing God's will than doing evil! God bless and much love.

# Daily Devotions

---

Good morning! Read Isaiah 46:9–10 and 2 Corinthians 5:7. One of the greatest fears that we all face from time to time is the fear of the unknown. Not knowing what the next year will bring or next month or next week or even how today will unfold. Often feeling blind to what lies ahead! However, you can replace your fears of the unknown with faith in God who knows the end from the beginning! It's by having the eyes of faith that we face all of our todays and tomorrows, knowing God sees all things! God bless and much love.

# Daily Devotions

———◆❖◆———

Good morning! Read Romans 14:1–12. Many have many opinions on ways to serve God. Judging others if their opinions and beliefs are different than theirs. From the ways to praise and worship God to what to eat and not to eat. What's most important to God is that we regard each day unto Him and give Him thanks in all things. It's not what we do or don't do but rather or not it's unto God with sincerity of the heart! God receives all who receive Him! It's His opinion that matters! Judgment is in His hands! God bless and much love.

# Daily Devotions

G ood morning! Read 2 Timothy 3:1–7. The Apostle Paul wrote and prophesied of the last days two thousand years ago. Days we are living in today. The mistrust and lack of concern for others and surrounded by codes and conspiracies that have created doubt and uncertainties in the minds of many. Searching for truth but not able to find it! However, it's knowing the truth of God that prepares you for the days ahead! To face each day with faith knowing God is with you in these last days! God bless and much love.

# Daily Devotions

———◆◆◆———

Good morning! Read 1 Samuel 30:6 and 1 Corinthians 15:57, then Galatians 6:9. There comes a time in life when we are hit by discouragement, fear, and doubt. Seeing the door God has opened for us but we are hesitant to go through. Much like the Israelites hesitation at crossing the Red Sea. During these times, we can find strength and encouragement in God who gives us strength and direction. Understanding that we are victorious in Christ and hold the Word of God as our staff to part our Red Sea of life that we may cross over. God bless and much love.

# Daily Devotions

---

Good morning! Read Romans 12:1–2 and 2 Corinthians 3:15–18. When we submit our lives to God a change begins to happen. Moreover, it's more than just a change, but it's a transitional and transformational change! Creating in you a new you to completely fulfill the plan God has for you! However, God cannot and will not make the change in you if you're not willing to change! It's by your humility and submission and acceptance of God that opens the door of your heart for God to begin His work in you! God bless and much love.

# Daily Devotions

———◇◆◇◆◇———

Good morning! Read Job 42:10–17 and Isaiah 59:1 and 61:7, then John 10:10. The devil is out to take away everything that we have. To destroy our hope and crush our faith. To divide families and separate us from what we are intended to have in Christ Jesus. But God is faithful to restore and multiply what the devil has taken away. Whatever the situation the devil has put us in, God can fix it! Keep believing, keep hoping, and keep trusting! God bless and much love.

# Daily Devotions

---

Good morning! Read Ezekiel 11:19–21. Reckless driving is dangerous to everyone driving including the reckless driver themselves. It's showing a lack of self-control and respect to the other drivers and shows a lack of self-respect for themselves. There are many who lack control and live reckless lives, unable to yield to caution but tossing caution to the wind. However, yielding to God's Word can change anyone. From a life of disrespect to being respectful. From the depths of uncontrollability to being in complete control. God bless and much love.

# Daily Devotions

———◇◈◇◈◇———

Good morning! Read Psalm 91:1–6. It's never nice to be locked outside in the cold and rain. It's much better to be inside enjoying the warmth in front of a cozy fireplace. Living a life without God is like being outside in the cold and rain. There's nothing to protect you from the elements. Living a life in the will of God is like being on the inside enjoying the warmth of that cozy fireplace. You find relaxation from the stress of everyday life and a sense of protection and peace. Are you living on the outside or on the inside? God bless and much love.

# Daily Devotions

---

Good morning! Read Jeremiah 31:34 and Philippians 2:5–11. There are times when we know of someone but don't know them personally. There are many that know of God but don't have a personal relationship with Him. Only by knowing someone can you begin to build a personal relationship with them. Only by knowing God can you build a relationship with Him that will grow. Whether you know God or not, the day will come when everyone will know Him and every knee will bow and confess Jesus Christ! God bless and much love.

# Daily Devotions

———◇◇◇◇◇———

Good morning! Read John 8:12. It's very difficult to walk and move around in the dark. Without seeing where you're going in the dark can cause you to stumble and run into things. It's necessary to have light to see your way around and through where you are to get to where you need to be safely. Thank and praise God for sending Jesus Christ to be the Light that shines in a darkened world! That we are guided by the Light of Christ around and through the darkened path of this life! There is no darkness in Him! God bless and much love.

# Daily Devotions

---

Good morning! Read Proverbs 4:20–27. Self-care is important! To change your physical appearance, you must change how you treat your body and what you put in your body. Our appearance is often a result of our self-care! Our heart and mind also requires self-care! To change your heart and mind, you must change what you allow into your heart and mind! What goes in your heart and mind is evident in what comes out of your heart and mind! Be mindful of your self-care! It's evidence of who you are! God bless and much love.

# Daily Devotions

———◇◇◇◇———

Good morning! Read Galatians 5:13–25 and Hebrews 6:4–6. When we come to Christ, we are given freedom in Christ. This does not mean that we have the liberty to live our lives as we did before we came to Christ. Coming to Christ brings change in how we feel, act, and think. If you are sincere, you will seek to be Christ-like in every aspect of your life. To fall back into your old ways are met with serious consequences from God Himself. God bless and much love.

# Daily Devotions

---

Good morning! Read Matthew 7:21–27 (emphasis on verse 21) and John 14:23–24. There are many that profess their Christianity and their love for God but neglect to do the will of God. Basking in their own righteousness and self-will and omitting the righteousness and will of God. Being deceived not knowing the judgment that one day awaits us all. To love God is to live according to the Word of God. Any other option is to bring God down to your level instead of rising to the level of what the Word of God says. It's God's will be done! God bless and much love.

# Daily Devotions

———◇◇◇◇◇◇———

Good morning! Read 1 Kings 3:5 and 9–13 and Proverbs 8:11–12, then James 1:5–8. If you had a wish list, what would be on that list? Material things? Riches? Long life? What about godly wisdom? Is there a place for the wisdom of God on your list that can lead and direct you that you may be satisfied and content in your life? That you may be able to discern and make the right decisions to lead you to where you want to be? The value of the wisdom of God outweighs anything you could ever want or imagine! God bless and much love.

# Daily Devotions

———◇◆◇———

Good morning! Read Proverbs 3:5–7. There are times God delays our deliverance from certain crises because of our need for our spiritual development in Him. There are times God will not remove certain problems in our life but will give us the strength to push through them. This also is for our spiritual development in Him. Our development in God is a process. It's important for us to trust the process and to trust God! God will never leave us nor forsake us! God knows what's He's doing! Trust Him! God bless and much love.

# Daily Devotions

———✦✦✦———

Good morning! Read Philippians 4:11–13 and 1 Timothy 6:6–12. There is much contentment in living a life in Christ. You're never too high or too low but are content in spite of what's happening around you. Understanding that godliness with contentment is great gain! Avoiding the trap of the love of money and material wealth that can draw you from the faith that has brought you the contentment you've found in Christ. Continuing to fight the good fight of faith that leads you to eternal life in Christ Jesus! God bless and much love.

# Daily Devotions

---

Good morning! Read Galatians 6:7–9. Each season has its purpose. There is a season to plant seeds and a season to reap the harvest of what has been planted. However, to have a successful harvest of what has been planted, it must be properly nourished. Every season is the season to plant the seed of the Word of God into your heart! Like all seeds, if it's nourished, it will bring forth a harvest of blessings from God into your life! Sometimes the waiting may be long, but it's definitely worth the wait! Be patient! God bless and much love.

# Daily Devotions

———◇◇◇◇◇◇———

Good morning! Read Psalm 119:9–16 and Proverbs 9:10. God's Word is a guide book to direct our steps along the road to salvation. It contains the dos and don'ts to keep us out of harm's way. To equip us with His wisdom and love to live a life pleasing to Him that in return we may be complete in Him. Only through His Word do we get knowledge and understanding to open our eyes to what we don't understand. But you must read the book! God bless and much love.

# Daily Devotions

---

Good morning! Read Matthew 5:14–16. In a world that is darkened by violence, sin, sickness, etc., the only hope is the Light of God. We, as followers of Christ, reflect the Light of God to the world. Darkness and light cannot coexist together. The same as having your eyes opened or closed. You only see the light through eyes that are open. As children of God, our light shines through our good works and our good works are to glorify God. To bring others out of darkness into the light that all may experience the mercy and grace of God. God bless and much love.

# Daily Devotions

---

Good morning! Read Psalm 12:6 and Isaiah 55:11, then Hebrews 4:12. When God speaks, He speaks to the heart. It's important that our heart is prepared to be pure and humble to receive the pure words of God. Whatever is spoken by God will not return to Him void but will accomplish what He has said. However, to receive and grow in the Word of God you must first receive Him! By receiving Him is when you get to know Him! Only then can you experience the power of the living Word of God! God bless and much love.

# Daily Devotions

---

Good morning! Read Nehemiah 8:10 and Galatians 5:22–25. The devil is always trying to steal our joy. When we keep our joy in God the fruit of the Spirit will bear much fruit in our lives. We lose our joy when we look for joy outside of God! To find joy in material things or others is temporary and cannot compare to the fruit of the Spirit that only God can provide. It's by keeping our joy in God, that continuously flows, do we find the peace and serenity that we desire! Live in the joy of the Lord! God bless and much love.

# Daily Devotions

---

Good morning! Read Acts 26:16–18 and 2 Corinthians 5:19–21. We have representatives who are to serve in the best interests of the people. We have ambassadors who represent this country to other countries. Those called by God are ambassadors of Christ to the world! As ambassadors, we are to speak the words of God to open the eyes of the world to the goodness of God! To turn them from darkness to light and from the power of Satan unto God! As an ambassador of Christ, represent Him well! God bless and much love.

# Daily Devotions

---

Good morning! Read 1 Corinthians 8:8–13. We all have different thoughts and viewpoints on many different things. We all have different likes and dislikes about many different things and are different in many ways. However, we all can be the same in respect for one another! To respectfully respect others is not just the right thing to do, but it's the godly thing to do! No one likes or appreciates being offended and no one should be offensive to others! We are to love one another and not offend! God bless and much love.

# Daily Devotions

Good morning! Read Ezekiel 36:25–28 and John 14:23, then Hebrews 4:9–12. No one wants to move into a house where the previous tenants left things behind. For God to live inside of us we must empty ourselves of ourselves and seek to find rest in Him. Ceasing from our works to be one in body, soul, and spirit in Him. God not only wants to be our sole provider but our soul provider. To prepare us for the next phase in life. It's time to clean house! God bless and much love.

# Daily Devotions

———◆◆◆◆◆———

Good morning! Read Philippians 4:4–8. Every athlete knows the importance of getting off to a great start and having a great finish. Every business has this same concept for their employees. This maximizes our performance in any task we have at hand. As individuals, we should and need to have this same concept in our daily relationship with God. To begin our day and end our day with prayer. This will also maximize our performance with the favor of God working on our behalf. A great start leads to a great finish. Take the time to pray! God bless and much love.

# Daily Devotions

———◆◆◆◆———

G ood morning! Read Genesis 15:5–6. On a clear night, you can see the many stars in the heavens above. Yet there are many more stars so far away they cannot be seen. Even the stars we see are too many to count. The blessings of God over our lifetime are like the stars. Far too many to count. God's blessings are also like the stars we cannot see. He has blessed us in so many ways that we don't know and haven't seen. It's God's love for us that His blessings keep flowing in our lives! Praise Him! God bless and much love.

# Daily Devotions

―――◇◈◇◈◇――

Good morning! Read Mark 16:15–20. Jesus, in His gospel, spoke of the coming of the kingdom of God. Jesus also instructed us do likewise and to preach His gospel throughout the world to everyone of the coming kingdom of God. To do so you must believe in His gospel and be baptized in your heart! Only then can the power of God work in you and through you to accomplish the things that are according to God's will for you and those who hear and believe the words of the gospel of Christ! God bless and much love.

# Daily Devotions

———◇◆◇———

Good morning! Read Psalm 139:14–18. Our life is like a puzzle with many pieces that need to be put together. The good news is in the mind of God, all the pieces are already in place. The better news is the Holy Spirit is there to help us put the right pieces into its proper place. When our puzzle of life is complete, we also are complete in God! Having Christ as the centerpiece of your puzzle of life is the most important piece! Start with the centerpiece and work your way out! Let the Holy Spirit guide you! God bless and much love.

# Daily Devotions

---◇◈◇◈◇---

Good morning! Read 2 Timothy 1:7 and 1 John 4:18, then 3rd John verse 2. There are many who are paranoid and paralyzed by fear! The fear of what can go wrong as opposed to what has gone right! The fear of believing what they hear or have heard and not believing or knowing what God has said! It's knowing and living in the perfect love of God that drives out fear from your life. That you are not paranoid and paralyzed by fear but to be in good health and prosper in God's perfect love! Be free from fear! God bless and much love.

# Daily Devotions

---

Good morning! Read Deuteronomy 8:18 and 1 Chronicles 29:11–13, then 2 Corinthians 3:5. We all have lost something, but nothing is lost in the eyes of God. God sees all and knows all. We become lost when we turn away from God or refuse to look to God who is our source of strength and sufficiently and wealth. It is because of His mercy and grace that God supplies us with what we need. Seek His face for much needed face time! God bless and much love.

# Daily Devotions

---◇◇◇◇◇---

Good morning! Read Job 3:25 and Jeremiah 33:3. Procrastination is a problem many face or have faced. Putting off until later what can be and should be done. Knowing and having the thought of the outcome if we don't act. Only to find that what was once a thought has now become a reality. A reality that could have been prevented if we did not procrastinate. God can give you the needed motivation to get you back on track. God will answer the call and show you mighty things as He turns your life around. But you must make the call! God bless and much love.

# Daily Devotions

———◇◇◇———

Good morning! Read Exodus 23:20–22 and Proverbs 3:5–6. Like a ship lost at sea, there are times in life when we feel lost with no direction. Wandering aimlessly through life searching and waiting for the direction we need to reach our desired promised land. During these times is when we must look to God and put our life and trust in His hands. To be committed to Him in all our ways. When we do, our path will be established, and His direction will become clear. God will lead us and guide us along the way! God bless and much love.

# Daily Devotions

———◆◆◆———

Good morning! Read Exodus 23:20–22 and Proverbs 3:5–6. Like a ship lost at sea, there are times in life when we feel lost with no direction. Wandering aimlessly through life searching and waiting for the direction we need to reach our desired promised land. During these times is when we must look to God and put our life and trust in His hands. To be committed to Him in all our ways. When we do, our path will be established, and His direction will become clear. God will lead us and guide us along the way! God bless and much love.

# Daily Devotions

———◇◆◇◆◇———

Good morning! Read Romans 1:16. Anytime we purchase anything with accessories that must be assembled, it comes with instructions. A new car comes with a car manual to help us understand the various parts of how the car works. Unless we follow the instructions, we don't understand how they work. God has given us His Word to give us instructions of how to live. However, if we don't follow the instructions, we cannot understand. Who else can teach us about life but God who gave us life? God bless and much love.

# Daily Devotions

---

Good morning! Read Ecclesiastes 7:25 and John 6:37. When we apply for employment, we hope to be accepted and hired to do the work. We hope to be accepted by our friends and peers. To be rejected can be emotionally hurtful. However, when we apply our heart to God, we will be accepted by Him. God will in no wise cast out anyone that comes to Him. When we come to God, God's plan for us begins to unfold in our lives. It's important that you *do not* resist the plan God has for you! Trust Him! God bless and much love.

# Daily Devotions

---

Good morning! Read Genesis 39:21–23 and 45:5–8 and 50:19–20, then Romans 8:28. Whenever we're in difficult and unfortunate circumstances, God can and will show His mercy and favor when we look to Him for comfort and contentment. God can also flip the script on those who wish to do you harm! Turning what they meant to harm you into a blessing for you! God can and will even use the devil himself to accomplish His plan for your life! All things work together for good when you love God! God bless and much love.

# Daily Devotions

---

Good morning! Read Psalm 107:29–38 and Jeremiah 29:11–13. God reigns in heaven and earth. Nothing happens unless God allows it to happen. God holds the future and God lives in us. Therefore, God holds our future and gives us quietness in the midst of the storms around us, shielding us from all harm to accomplish what He already has pre-destined for us. To give us an expected end and fulfilling every promise He has made in His Word. God bless and much love.

# Daily Devotions

---

Good morning! Read Numbers 23:19 and Isaiah 65:24, then Hebrews 11:6. Those who love God have a longing to hear from God. Patiently waiting with hope and faith to receive the many promises of God. God also has a longing to hear from those who love Him to fulfill the promises He has made. If God has said it, He is able to bring it to pass. However, the fulfilling of His promises are conditional. Having a sincere heart toward God and obedience to His Word are what pleases God. Being strong in faith as we diligently seek Him. God bless and much love.

# Daily Devotions

Good morning! Read Matthew 24:35 and 2 Timothy 4:6–8. We all have memories of friends and loved ones who have passed on. Some memories of some are good, and some are not so good. One day we will be a memory for our loved ones and friends. The question is, how do you want to be remembered? As someone who was loving or who was selfish and filled with hate? As someone who fought the good fight for Christ or someone who denied His faith? Remember, memories last long after we're gone! God bless and much love.

# Daily Devotions

---

Good morning! Read James 4:5–10. There are many who can accomplish many things. To accomplish anything takes work and the knowledge of what's being accomplished. The most difficult thing to accomplish is having the ability to resist evil! God's plan to resist evil is by submitting yourself to Him. It's by submitting yourself to God do you begin to gain the knowledge of God and strength to resist evil. All evil is of the devil! When you resist the devil, he will flee from you, and God will lift you up! God bless and much love.

# Daily Devotions

---

Good morning! Read Acts 17:11 and Colossians 2:6–10, then 2 Timothy 2:15. Whenever we're given any information, it's always wise to have confirmation for what has been done. Getting a receipt when paying a bill or getting a confirmation number in completing an online transaction. When we hear a teacher of the Word of God, we should also confirm their teaching with the Word of God itself. That you are not deceived by anything taken out of context! Study! Don't be deceived! God bless and much love.

# Daily Devotions

---

Good morning! Read Psalm 11:7 and Hebrews 11:6 and 12:2. God is righteous, and we are righteous in God because of our faith in God. Our faith is established when we believe in God and have put our trust in Him. Without believing, your faith has no foundation, and you cannot build your faith without a foundation for your faith! And that foundation must be built on Jesus Christ who is the author and finisher of our faith! It's by our faith and through our faith we are righteous before God who is righteous! God bless and much love.

# Daily Devotions

Good morning! Read 2 Chronicles 14:11 and Proverbs 18:10, then Isaiah 54:17 and Philippians 4:13. The hand of God is strength to all who call on His name. Whether our problems are few or many, God is a stronghold to all who believe in Him and the power of His might. God promises that no weapon that is formed against thee shall prosper. When our strength fails, the power of God will strengthen us in all we undertake. God bless and much love.

# Daily Devotions

---

Good morning! Read Psalm 34:8, then Romans 8:29 and 12:1–2. It's God's desire to conform us into the image of His Son. Be Christlike in the manner in which we live our life. This is not possible if we are conformed to the ways of the world. It takes a transformation by the renewing of the mind. To close the door to who we have been and to open the door to who God will enable us to become. To open that door, we must open the Bible, which is His Word. A closed mouth doesn't get fed! Open wide and taste the goodness of God! God bless and much love.

# Daily Devotions

———◇◈◇◈◇———

G ood morning! Read Joshua 1:5–9. Every true believer in God has their confidence and faith in the mighty power of God. Knowing He is always there to comfort us and give us the strength needed to make it through each day. But the question is, can God be confident and depend on you? To faithfully speak on His behalf and live your life in His strength as an example for others to see? To be courageous in your walk and to observe to do what God has said? Can you truly say that God can depend on you! God bless and much love.

# Daily Devotions

———◇◇◇◇◇◇———

Good morning! Read Deuteronomy 30:10–20 and John 14:6. Any direction we go in life, we take it step by step. What's important is that we take the right direction when we take our steps. There is one direction in life that leads to God. Any other direction leads from God. The direction to God is not far but is always near. God is not to high nor to low that God cannot be reached. God is always at hand! The direction to God is the direction to life! The direction to God is found in the pathway of Jesus Christ! God bless and much love.

# Daily Devotions

---

Good morning! Read 1 Samuel 30:6 and Psalm 23:4. The storms of life can challenge your faith in God. What's important is how you respond to the challenge when you are faced with the storms of life. Do you give in and fold to the storms of life, or do you encourage yourself in the Lord? It's by encouraging yourself in God that your fears are overcome by your faith! It's by encouraging yourself in God that your doubts are cast down knowing God is with you during your storms of life! God bless and much love.

# Daily Devotions

———— ◇◇◇◇◇◇ ————

Good morning! Read 1 Corinthians 10:13 and James 1:12–16, then 2 Peter 2:9. We all face various trials and temptations from time to time. Being enticed and lured into situations and circumstances we often try to avoid. However, it's standing strong and enduring the various trials and temptations that strengthens our faith and character! More importantly, it's knowing God is there to assist us in providing an outlet that we may escape. But it's our responsibility to take advantage of the outlet God has provided! God bless and much love.

# Daily Devotions

———✦✦✦———

Good morning! Read 2 Peter 1:3–10. God has given us all things that pertain unto life and godliness! As you go deeper into the knowledge of God, your awareness and understanding of God grows. Like a set of building blocks, you are building yourself up in the things of God. From the growing of your faith to learning patience to having kindness and love and respect to others. You are building your life to be fully equipped to living a life that is rewarded and blessed by God! God bless and much love.

# Daily Devotions

———— ❖ ————

Good morning! Read Psalm 14:1–7 and 91:1–5. God is good! All that truly believe and truly trust know and can witness to the goodness of God. God refers to all who don't believe in Him in their heart as being a fool. God is righteous and faithful to the faithful and a shelter and refuge to all that seek Him with a pure heart. His rewards cannot be counted or measured which He willingly gives to all who are obedient to His Word. Aligning their will according to His will. God bless and much love.

# Daily Devotions

---

Good morning! Read Psalm 34:6–8, then 40:1–5 and 8–11. When we put our trust and faith in God, we patiently wait and hope, having expectation that God hears our prayers and will answer our prayers in due time. God has put a new song in our hearts that others may see and hear. A song that testifies to the amazing grace of God to all who humble themselves and call upon His name. To find delight in doing His will and refreshing and giving rest to a weary soul. To be renewed with His strength day by day. God bless and much love.

# Daily Devotions

***

Good morning! Read Isaiah 43:1–2 and 59:1. Often it's hard to understand why certain things and circumstances happen to us. However, those who are of God understand that whatever happens to us is for us so God can continue His work within us! There's a reason for everything God allows us to go through. What we don't understand now will be revealed to us in time. It's important to continually trust in the power of God to save and deliver us during times of our uncertainty! God bless and much love.

# Daily Devotions

---

Good morning! Read Romans 12:1–2 and Philippians 4:8. Wrong thinking fuels wrong ideas that lead you in the wrong direction. But right thinking fuels right ideas that lead you in the right direction. It's by renewing your mind with the things of God that leads you down the path of righteousness to think right things that are right and true in the eyes of God. However, the decision to be transformed in the mind unto God begins with you! Have you made the right or the wrong decision? Your life depends on it! God bless and much love.

# Daily Devotions

———⟨⟩⟨⟩⟨⟩———

Good morning! Read Romans 15:4 and 1 Corinthians 10:11–12. It's often said, if you don't know your history, you're doomed to repeat it! There is truth to this statement! The Bible is a history book detailing the history of God's creation and His relationship with His children. Their mistakes and God's form of correction of those mistakes are lessons for us to learn so we don't make similar mistakes. We learn from our mistakes, and we also learn from the mistakes of others! Know and understand your history! Know God! God bless and much love.

# Daily Devotions

———◆◆◆———

Good morning! Read Joshua 1:5–9 and John 10:10, then Ephesians 3:16–21. Satan is an adversary to God. Not only to God, but to all that seek God and all that have become the children of God. Overshadowing our lives with fear. Although we may feel this fear, we don't have to be afraid. Just as the sun burns away the clouds, our persistent faith in God will enable us to overcome all fear. It's God's command that we be strong and courageous. God bless and much love.

# Daily Devotions

---

Good morning! Read John 10:10 and 1 John 2:16–17. A spider spins a web to trap its prey. To devour it when it's ready. The devil spins a web of lies, deceit, fear, doubt, and false rewards to trap his prey. To eventually devour over time. To avoid being caught in the devil's web, you must recognize the devices that the devil uses. The lust of the flesh, and the lust of the eyes, and the pride of life! Seeing and hearing in the Spirit of God will enable you to avoid being entrapped in the devil's web! God bless and much love.

# Daily Devotions

———◇◇◇◇◇———

G ood morning! Read Psalm 136:1–6 and Mark 12:29–31. We give a thank you whenever someone does something nice for us. We expect a thank you whenever we do something nice. We consider it rude when we are not given thanks and can feel offended. How often do you give God thanks for the things He has done? God deserves a thank you each day and throughout the day for life itself. Just as we give thanks and expect thanks from others, let's give God the highest form of thanks which is our heart, soul, mind, and strength. God bless and much love.

# Daily Devotions

———✦✦✦———

Good morning! Read 1 Corinthians 1:23–31 and 2:12–16. For any job we do, we must be equipped to do the job. To be successful in school, we must be equipped with what's been taught in the classroom. God has equipped His children to be successful in living a spiritual life. To know and understand the ways of God that the unbelievers in God doesn't understand. It's the wisdom and strength of God that brings confusion to those who don't understand God. But we understand because we are of God! God bless and much love.

# Daily Devotions

———◇◇◇◇———

G ood morning! Read Romans 10:13 and Philippians 4:5–7. We all go through some form of adversity from time to time. Whether it's our health, our finances, relationships, overcoming the passing of a loved one, etc., we need deliverance and pray to God to be saved from our hardship. However, it must be understood that often God's deliverance is giving you the strength to get through whatever you may be going through. That you may grow and mature in the understanding and knowledge of Him! God bless and much love.

# Daily Devotions

———◇◇◇◇———

Good morning! Read Psalm 12:6–7 and Hebrews 4:12. The Word of God is the Word of Truth! It's the spoken Word of God that has created everything in this world and everything that exist in the heavens above. The Word of God is powerful! It's the Word of God that powers life into each and every one of us. When we speak God's Word faithfully, it has the power to faithfully accomplish God's will! God has preserved His Word for us! The earth and heavens may pass away, but God's Word will stand forever! God bless and much love.

# Daily Devotions

———◈◈◈◈◈———

G ood morning! Read Luke 8:5–21. A farmer cultivates his land and makes sure it has the proper irrigation before he plants his crop. He removes all the rocks and weeds to ensure the crop is not hindered while its growing. He then plants the seeds and patiently waits for the crop to grow. We must be like this farmer in preparing our heart to receive the Word of God. Removing what hinders our spiritual growth and our irrigation system is the Word of God. God bless and much love.

# Daily Devotions

---

G ood morning! Read Psalm 1:1–6 and 1 Corinthians 15:33, then 2 Corinthians 6:14–18. The company we keep can determine who we become. If we walk in an area with the smell of smoke, that smell lingers on us. If we walk through a field of flowers, the scent of the flowers remains on us. The company we keep is no different. Bad ideas lead to bad actions. The righteousness of God and unrighteousness cannot fellowship together. To be good and do good, you must separate yourself from what's not good for you. God bless and much love.

# Daily Devotions

———◇◇◇◇———

Good morning! Read Romans 8:29–31 and Philippians 2:5. Many of us have spent many years of our life wondering what our purpose is in life. But if we look to God in prayer, our purpose will be revealed to us in time. God not only has a purpose for us, but our purpose was predestined in the mind of God before we came into being. That purpose was to be conformed to the image of His Son. That we may be justified and glorified in Him. Having the mind of Christ, we are confident in our purpose in Christ! God bless and much love.

# Daily Devotions

———◇◇◇◇◇◇———

Good morning! Read 2 Corinthians 6:14–18 and 2 Peter 2:19–22. You would never plant a rose among a bed of weeds because the weeds will choke out the life of the rose. A rose must be planted among other roses. A child of God who continuously associates with the ungodly are planting themselves among a bed of weeds! The spiritual life in them is slowly choked out! God has uprooted you from the bed of weeds of the world! It's foolish to replant yourself among them! God bless and much love.

# Daily Devotions

---

Good morning! Read Luke 10:30–37 and James 2:14–17. One of the most important lessons in the Bible is to love thy neighbor. Jesus taught about having the passion and compassion for one another. Passion is feeling and understanding what someone is going through, but to have compassion means you feel and understand and you do something about it! It's the working of our faith that gives us the compassion to extend our help to those in need. This is also an extension of the love of God! God bless and much love.

# Daily Devotions

———◇◇◇◇◇◇———

Good morning! Read 2 Timothy 2:15 and James 1:22–25. It is God's will that we come to the knowledge of Him. Only by reading and studying His Word can this be done. More importantly, to understand His Word, we must experience His Word. Having head knowledge is one thing, but to have the experience allows us to fully understand. You can read how to hit a baseball or shoot a basketball, but until you actually practice doing it, you don't know what it feels like doing it the right way. Put what God says into action in your life. God bless and much love.

# Daily Devotions

---

Good morning! Read Job 36:5–12 and Isaiah 55:8–11. Our God is mighty, and His thoughts and ways exceed our imaginations. When our ways and thoughts are in alignment with those of God, we are blessed in all we do. However, our disobedience has consequences. But God's discipline is not out of anger but because of the great love He has for us. To go against and disregard His correction is like trying to swim upstream. Only God's stream leads us to a bigger ocean that leads to His righteousness and pleasures of life. God bless and much love.

# Daily Devotions

———◇◈◇———

Good morning! Read Joshua 1:5–9 and Psalm 121:1–3, then Isaiah 43:18–19. Many live their life with expectations! Sadly, some have the mindset of "what else is going to go wrong?" But for those who believe God look to Him with unwavering faith! Understanding God can change any situation at any time! It's God that keeps us from falling while we wait for the expectation of a new thing from God! God has commanded us to keep moving forward because as we move forward, God is moving forward with us! God bless and much love.

# Daily Devotions

---

Good morning! Read Ephesians 1:4–12 and James 4:7–10. Every relationship begins with friendship, and in every friendship, there must be trust. God has had a relationship with His children from the beginning, but our relationship with Him begins when we submit our life to Him. By doing so, our relationship is built and begins to grow because of the growing trust in Him. This trust fuels our faith, and our faith draws us closer to Him. Our relationship with God is the most important relationship we can have! God bless and much love.

# Daily Devotions

---

Good morning! Read Zechariah 1:3. If you are driving and miss your turn, you must make a U-turn to get back to your desired destination. The farther you drive, the farther you have to drive back! If you have been backsliding in your relationship with God, you have to make a U-turn to get back to Him! It's by reconciliation in your relationship with God that God is reconciled to you. But you must turn unto God that God may turn unto you and set you back on the destination He has for you in life! God bless and much love.

# Daily Devotions

---

Good morning! Read Joshua 1:8–9. The more we read a book, the more we understand the book. The more we understand the laws and rules of society, the more we are able to live within those laws and rules. When we understand the Word of God, we are more conscious of what's acceptable to God and what is not. However, it's by living according to God's Word that paves the way to living a life that is pleasing to God. To living a life that is blessed and prosperous and successful in ways that are beyond our imagination! God bless and much love.

# Daily Devotions

---

Good morning! Read Romans 10:17 and Hebrews 11:1–6–10 and 17–20. The birthplace of our faith is by hearing the Word of God. Our faith is increased by overcoming the trials and tests God allows us to go through. Many times taking us to the limit where we see no way out. This is when our faith is proven. Not to God, but to us! God knows what we need and when we need it. God wouldn't bring you this far to leave you in times of testing. Increase daily in faith and stand tall and firm in your faith. Believe! God bless and much love.

# Daily Devotions

———◇◈◇———

Good morning! Read John 14:12. Jesus told His followers, "He that believeth on me, the works that I do shall he do also and greater works than these shall he do." What greater works can we do who believe? We have the capability through technology to reach the entire world. During the time of Jesus, this was not possible. He could only speak His gospel to those in the regions where He traveled. We have been ordained through the Holy Spirit to spread His message to the entire world. The question is not *can* you, but *will* you? God bless and much love.

# Daily Devotions

G ood morning! Read John 11:40–45 and
Ephesians 5:20. Having trust and faith
in God is displayed in our giving of thanks
before, during, and after God has given us
deliverance from what we pray for. Jesus
Christ is the perfect example to follow! Many
of the miracles done (as feeding thousands
with a few loads of bread and a few fish or
raising Lazarus from the dead) Jesus gave
thanks to God *before* the miracles were done.
Having continuous giving of thanks to God is
important in our deliverance! God bless and
much love.

# Daily Devotions

---

Good morning! Read Galatians 1:10. Everyone wants to be accepted and loved by their peers. For some, they go along to get along, even though they see the wrong in doing so, laying aside their integrity and dignity in the process to be accepted. Anyone in Christ knows and understands the One whose acceptance and approval that is important is that of God. God's approval will keep your integrity and dignity intact and strengthen you to live in His truth and lead others to His truth as well! God bless and much love.

# Daily Devotions

---

Good morning! Read Psalm 55:21–23. Deceitful people use deceitful words to deceive others for their own profit. Their words are smoother than butter and softer than oil as they attempt to deceive others. It's by turning your life over to God who knows the intents of the heart of each of us that the deceiver is exposed! God is your protection from all who would attempt to deceive others. However, it's important that you put the burden of deceit into His hands! More importantly, trust God! God bless and much love.

# Daily Devotions

———◇◇◇◇———

Good morning! Read Malachi 3:8–10. Tithing is important! However, tithing goes far beyond the giving of your finances. It's also 10 percent of your time! It's not weekly or monthly giving but a daily giving of your time to the studying of God's Word and being of service to God and others. There are twenty-four hours in a day! God is pleased and will add blessings to you for giving 10 percent of your day to Him! What you give in the service to God and for God is multiplied in blessings back to you! Give and it shall be given! God bless and much love.

# Daily Devotions

———◇◇◇◇◇◇◇———

Good morning! Read Mark 16:15–20 and Hebrews 13:8, then Revelation 1:8. By tomorrow, today's current events will be yesterday's news. Everything we see and do will fade and become a memory as time passes. The only thing that has stood the test of time and is always current is the Word of God and what is says about those who believe. Only God has no beginning and no end. What Jesus declared then applies to us now! His Gospel declares who we are, and His promise of the Holy Spirit is here today and forever. God bless and much love.

# Daily Devotions

---✦✦✦---

Good morning! Read Matthew 6:7–15 and Mark 11:22–26 (emphasis on verse 24). Jesus gave us an outline on how to pray, giving God honor and expressing our wants and needs and seeking God's direction. To forgive others to be forgiven ourselves. Jesus also has taught us to live a life with expectation. Having expectation based on our faith in God. Believing God will answer our prayers and to live our life accordingly. Being thankful and showing our thankfulness by being obedient to His Word. God bless and much love.

# Daily Devotions

———◇◇◇◇◇———

Good morning! Read 1 Corinthians 9:24–27 and Philippians 3:13–14. When an artist looks at an empty canvas, they don't see an empty canvas, but they see a finished picture of what they are going to paint. Likewise, a runner sees the prize to be won at the end of the race. Neither one sees what is but what the end result can be. God sees the finished works of the canvas of our lives. Willing to give us the prize for the race in life we've run. The artist must paint, and the runner must run to achieve the desired success. We also must actively strive ahead in Christ! God bless and much love.

# Daily Devotions

———◈◈◈———

Good morning! Read Romans 5:1–5. We are justified by our faith in God. It's because of our faith that gives us peace with God. It's also because of our faith in God that we have hope. It's because of our hope in God, we still have joy and praise God during times of tribulations. Through times of tribulations, we learn patience. Throughout this patience, we gain the experience needed to prepare us for what God has prepared for us as we live our lives. It all begins with faith in God and that faith fuels our hope! God bless and much love.

# Daily Devotions

———◇❖◇———

Good morning! Read Romans 3:23 and 6:23, then 1 John 1:5–10. No one is perfect! We all have sinned and made mistakes. However, the biggest sin and mistake is not admitting your sin and/or mistake. Your denial is not only you lying to yourself, but it's also a lie before God! It's by admitting when we fall short that we are forgiven and cleansed by God of our unrighteousness and given a new start to begin again. Although we are not perfect, be thankful we serve a God who is perfect! God bless and much love.

# Daily Devotions

---

Good morning! Read 2 Peter 1:20–21. The Bible is simply amazing! Written over a span of approximately 1,500 years containing sixty-six books written by forty different writers inspired by God who were moved by the Holy Ghost to speak the words of God! We learn of the wrath of God toward disobedience and how the blessings of God are showered on those who are obedient! More importantly, from Genesis through Revelation is the common thread of Jesus Christ and God's love for us! God bless and much love.

# Daily Devotions

———◇◇◇———

Good morning! Read Psalm 27:14 and Romans 5:1–5, then James 1:2–4. We are familiar with the phrase "haste makes waste." Yet many live a life of rush, rush, rush! Never exceeding in the fashion they would like. Not understanding that patience leads to sound judgment and decision making in our daily affairs. Waiting for God's counsel relieves the stress and anxiety associated with a fast-paced lifestyle. God allows us to go through some tribulation to learn patience. This experience strengthens our faith and gives us hope. God bless and much love.

# Daily Devotions

---

Good morning! Read Romans 8:31 and Ephesians 6:10–17, then 1 John 4:1–6. There has been an ongoing spiritual battle for thousands of years. This battle affects each and every one today. The fight is strongest against the children of God. Satan and his angels are set to divide and conquer those chosen by God. But if the Word of God abides and lives in you, God Himself abides and lives in you, and you have the power to prevail over the enemies of God. But you must be prepared and stay prepared! God bless and much love.

# Daily Devotions

Good morning! Read Jeremiah 29:11–13 and Romans 10:9–13. Many use a daily planner to plan their day. Planning is important in much of what we do. Whether it's a wedding, our school curriculum, our job, etc., planning is important to reach our desired result. It's so important to understand the plan God has for each one of us. His plan of salvation that all can be saved. Salvation is found by accepting Jesus Christ as your Savior. Like any plan, if you don't follow the steps, your plan will fail! Follow God's plan and be saved! God bless and much love.

# Daily Devotions

———✦———

G ood morning! Read Acts 17:24–30 and
Romans 15:4–6. It's known and believed
by many that if we don't learn from our lessons of the past, we are doomed to repeat
them. The Bible is filled with lessons of failure and lessons of success by many from the
past. All these are lessons for us living today
to live by. It's the lessons learned that give us
hope! To ignore the lessons of the past is the
path to repeat the same lessons. At times of
this ignorance God winked at; but now com-
mands everyone to repent! Today is the day!
God bless and much love.

# Daily Devotions

———◇◇◇◇◇◇———

Good morning! Read John 1:12 and Romans 8:14–17, then 1 John 2:4–6. To be a child of God, you must first believe in God. You must also believe in His Son, Jesus Christ, and receive Him as your personal Savior. It's by believing and receiving that empowers you to live and walk in the Spirit of God and become an adopted child of God. If you know Him and believe in Him, you will be obedient to His Word. If you're obedient to His Word, then God in Christ and through Christ lives in you and you live in Him! God bless and much love.

# Daily Devotions

———◇❖◇———

Good morning! Read Matthew 13:30 and 25:32–46. We are living in the last days. Each day draws us closer to the day of harvest when the wheat of Christ will be separated from the tares. When the sheep of Christ are separated from the goats. The question is, are you a part of the wheat or part of the tares? One of the sheep or one of the goats? It's important to consider that whichever you are a part of has eternal rewards or eternal consequences! Hint: the rewards are far better! God bless and much love.

# Daily Devotions

———◇◇◇◇◇———

Good morning! Read Psalm 95:6–11 and Matthew 6:31–34, then Hebrews 4:7–11. There are many that say they don't have time for God. Or they say things like "I want to live my life first" or "maybe next year" or "next month" or "next week" or "tomorrow." Not understanding that tomorrow is not promised. It's God's will to save all and that all find rest in Him. But first, you must believe God can and will do what He says. To put God off day after day, the day will come when they're one day too late. Make today the day! God bless and much love.

# Daily Devotions

---

Good morning! Read Psalm 121:1–5 and 2 Corinthians 12:7–10. After each long hard day, our body requires rest and sleep to prepare itself for what's ahead the next day. This is a natural occurrence for everyone. For that little extra, why not turn to the One who requires no sleep or rest and has continuous power to strengthen you. To turn your natural into what's supernatural. To be your strength in times of weakness and to bring light in your hour of darkness. Having the power of God in Christ resting upon you. God bless and much love.

# Daily Devotions

———◇◇◇———

Good morning! Read Matthew 6:25–34 and 7:7. There are different sizes and shapes to all of us. It's also true that there are different problems and concerns that are different for each individual. What is common is that many are constantly searching for an answer to the cure of their problems and concerns. When you allow God to be active in your life, your problems and concerns because God's problems and concerns. Allow God to be the defining cure in your life. With God, one size fits all! God bless and much love.

# Daily Devotions

———◆◇◆◇◆———

Good morning! Read Psalm 138:2 and John 6:63 and Romans 1:16. God is real and alive, and His Word is real and alive and *should not* be taken lightly! To take the Word of God lightly is to take God lightly! For God has "magnified thy word above thy name." The Word of God is spirit and life and gives life to all who believe and receive it. The Word of God is the power of God unto salvation to everyone that believes! Therefore, believe and unashamed of the Word of God and live life in the spirit through His Word! God bless and much love.

# Daily Devotions

---

Good morning! Read Matthew 5:13. Much of the food we eat, we season with salt to bring out the flavor of the food to enhance its taste. God has seasoned His children with the salt of His Word to enhance our life so the words we speak are seasoned with the salt of His Word to enhance the lives of all who hear and receive His Word! However, if you haven't been seasoned with salt yourself by God's Word, how can you season the life of someone else? Let the salt of God's Word season your life! God bless and much love.

# Daily Devotions

G ood morning! Read Deuteronomy 29:9
Ecclesiastes 12:13–14, then Micah 6:8.
We like to be rewarded for what we do. At
work, we want to be paid for the work we
do. At school, we want our grades to reflect
the long hours of study we put into learning
a specific subject. We also want to be fairly
paid and fairly graded. What's fair to us may
not seem fair to the one paying us or grading
us, but one thing is certain: God is fair to all!
His judgment is just. If you don't agree, the
problem is not God but you. God bless and
much love.

# Daily Devotions

———◇◆◇◆◇———

Good morning! Read 2 Corinthians 11:24–30 and 12:7–10. When we accept Jesus Christ as our Savior, the enemy, Satan, steps up his attacks. There may be times when things turn out wrong that we think we are doing something wrong. Don't lose heart! It's not that we are doing something wrong, but that we are doing something right! The devil will always try to break you down in your pursuit of Christ. It's not our strength, but His strength that will cause you to overcome the workings of the devil. What Satan breaks down, God in Christ will rebuild. God bless and much love.

# Daily Devotions

---

Good morning! Read Deuteronomy 30:15–19 and Joshua 24:15. God *is not* responsible for your life if you choose to live your life apart from God. But God *is* responsible when you choose to live your life in Him. To seek Him with all that lies within you that you may receive all that God has planned specifically for you. Living a life apart from God leads to eventually certain death. Living your life in God leads to eventual everlasting life in the kingdom of God. The choice is yours! What is it? God bless and much love.

# Daily Devotions

---

Good morning! Read Proverbs 3:5–7 and Jeremiah 29:11–13, then Romans 8:28. We don't know what a year will bring. We don't know what will the next month or week or even the next day will bring...but God knows! God knows the end from the beginning in the lives of everyone! However, if we keep our trust in God and rely on His direction and understanding, all will be well. Let's not look at our circumstances but look to God for the unfolding of what we don't see or understand! God bless and much love.

# Daily Devotions

———◇✕✕◇———

Good morning! Read 2 Corinthians 12:7–10. Tragic events happen somewhere in the world often. Whether it's severe weather conditions, earthquakes, or some other natural event often referred to as an act of God" God may allow these things to happen, but He is not the cause! God heals He does not inflict tragic events! Satan is behind these natural events! However, God uses what the devil has done as an alter call to bring us unto Him for comfort! It's at the alter where we find strength in God! God bless and much love.

# Daily Devotions

———◇◈◇◈◇———

Good morning! Read Joshua 24:15 and Matthew 6:24, then 1 Corinthians 10:21–23. There are many who profess to love God, yet they also desire to be accepted by their peers who may not love God. Living a life of living two lives! One unto God and one unto their peers! One life leading them in one direction and one life leading them in another. It's important that a choice is made! We should not attempt to serve both! Water and oil don't mix, and neither should we attempt to mix living two lives! God bless and much love.

# Daily Devotions

---◈◈◈◈◈---

Good morning! Read Romans 8:14–17 and Hebrews 12:5–13. Every parent wants the best for their children. We teach them right from wrong and discipline them when needed because we love them. We encourage them to know their family history and to take pride in who they are. Everything that we want for our children, God wants for His children. God disciplines and teaches and wants us to know who we are in Him. If you were in God's place, how would you view yourself? Thank God for His mercy and grace! God bless and much love.

# Daily Devotions

---

Good morning! Read Psalm 12:6 and 119:11, then Hebrews 4:12. God's Word is alive! When we speak His Word, His Word is put into action. Having His Word and not speaking His Word is the same as sitting in a car and not driving anywhere. You are just idling. Speaking God's Word is like putting the pedal to the metal. Things begin to happen, and the power of God begins to move in your life. But you must know His Word to speak His Word. Otherwise, it's like wanting to drive that car but not having the skills to do so. God bless and much love.

# Daily Devotions

———◇◆◇———

G ood morning! Read Genesis 12:1–3 and Romans 8:31. There are times in life when God will move us from one part of His vineyard to another. That we may leave the old behind because God has something new for us. With this comes new blessings to go with a new beginning. So that we are not only blessed but are a blessing to those we encounter. God is with all who are with us and against all who are against us. It's with faith and trust that we go where God leads us to be spiritually led and spiritually fed! God bless and much love.

# Daily Devotions

———◇◇◇◇◇———

Good morning! Read Matthew 11:28–30 and John 4:10–14, then Philippians 4:4–7. Many are beset with problems and concerns daily in their lives. Often dealing with lack but hoping for abundance to come their way. But to the wise that abundance that many seek is found in God! However, it must be understood that the abundance is an overflowing well of God's mercy and grace to sustain us daily in our lives. Only by learning of God do we understand the overflow that God has made available! God bless and much love.

# Daily Devotions

———◇◇◇◇◇———

G ood morning! Read 1 Thessalonians 4:13–18. One of the most difficult times to deal with in life is the loss of a loved one. Whether they're family or friend, we all go through a time of mourning. However, if you believe in God, you find comfort knowing that one day Christ will return and the dead in Christ shall rise first! Those that are alive and in Christ shall be caught up together with them in the clouds to meet the Lord in the air! It's knowing we will be together again that gives us comfort in our grief! God bless and much love.

# Daily Devotions

---

Good morning! Read 1 Corinthians 3:1–2 and Hebrews 5:12–14, then 1 Peter 2:1–3. Newborn babies have a desire to be fed milk. Milk has everything that a newborn needs to be healthy and grow. As they grow, they are able to eat other foods such as meats and vegetables. As we grow in Christ, we must desire the sincere milk of the word of God that we may grow. The more we grow in knowledge, we begin to desire the meat of the Word! That we may teach other newborns the principles of the truth of God! God bless and much love.

# Daily Devotions

---

Good morning! Read Matthew 7:13–14 and John 14:6. The advances in technology are growing at an alarming rate. What is new today is old by tomorrow. With GPS, we can locate and find our destination by the touch of the hand. Satellite coverage allows us to see any place on the planet in a matter of seconds. However, all this technology cannot give you or show you a faster way to God. There remains only one way and one path that leads to God. The road to salvation has not changed. It's only through Jesus Christ. God bless and much love.

# Daily Devotions

Good morning! Read Proverbs 5–8. Everyone knows their past and present. The wonderment and mystery are what lies ahead. Not only today but the days to come can be a blessing if we put our lives in the hands of God who knows the end from the beginning. God *is not* constrained by time but lives outside of time. Our past, present, and future are always in the present with God. Just as children trust the judgment and direction of their parents, we should trust the judgment and direction of God. God bless and much love.

# Daily Devotions

---

Good morning! Read Psalm 46:10 and Isaiah 26:3–4. Time is constantly moving. Too fast for some, and too slow for others. But when our life is in Christ, time is at a constant medium. Because our time is His time! Our wait is on God's timetable and not ours. We can be still and know that our life and the times of our life are in His hands. We find rest and peace knowing what we do; the timing is already in the mind of God. It's God who will lift us, but we must be prepared to be lifted. Are you prepared? God bless and much love.

# Daily Devotions

———◆◇◆◇◆———

Good morning! Read Isaiah 55:1–3 and 2 Corinthians 3:5, then Philippians 4:19. We live in a society that is very costly. Constant rising living expenses and health costs and miscellaneous costs that continuously rise make it difficult for many to live a life of contentment and joy. However, those who know God understand that God is the source and sufficiency for all our needs. What God has given and is willing to give is free! The only cost is submitting your life to Him! God bless and much love.

# Daily Devotions

G ood morning! Read Matthew 10:16. Each dawning of a new day is another opportunity to improve ourselves and to be better than we were the day before. However, every day has its challenges! The challenges of making the right choices and right decisions that affect us and those around us. As we enter each day, we must be as wise as serpents and harmless as doves! To be wise in our choices and to be gentle in our approach to all things that come our way while abiding in the peace of God! God bless and much love.

# Daily Devotions

---※◇◆◇※---

Good morning! Read Luke 11:33–36 and James 3:8–18. When that which is dirty is mixed with that which is clean, that which is clean becomes dirty. We have been cleansed by the blood of Christ and the Word of God. We have His light that shines within us. Light always chases away darkness. Let your light shine and don't invite or allow darkness to dim the light of God that shines within. This light is a gift and a blessing, whereas the darkness is a curse to what God has given. Be wise in God's wisdom. God bless and much love.

# Daily Devotions

———⟨⬦⬦⬦⟩———

Good morning! Read Numbers 23:19 and Joshua 3:13–17, then James 2:17–18 and 26. There are many who declare their faith but are reluctant to put their faith into motion. Waiting for God to act before they act. However, the reverse is how we prove our faith. An example is when the children of Israel crossed the Jordan River. God divided the river after they stepped into the river. Proving their belief and faith that God would do as He said. Having faith is one thing, but putting feet to your faith is what moves God. Show your faith by your works! God bless and much love.

# Daily Devotions

———◇◆◇———

Good morning! Read Romans 12:1–2. Whenever anyone wants change to happen, whether it's their physical appearance or a change in the way they think, it takes action on their part. If it's physical, you must change your diet and do what's physically necessary to change your appearance. Just thinking about it won't make it happen! Neither can you change the way you think if you keep feeding your mind the same thing. But you must transform your mind by renewing your mind. God can direct you when you look to Him! God bless and much love.

# Daily Devotions

———◇◇◇◇◇———

G ood morning! Read 2 Corinthians 4:14–18 and 5:17. Everyone gets excited when they get new shoes and/or new clothes. We get showered and cleaned up to wear our new outfit and new shoes. The most important new apparel we can wear is that provided by God! The shoes of the preparation of the gospel of Christ and to be clothed with the cloak of righteousness of God will never wear out or get old. It is new every day! That which is natural will fade and get old, but that which is of God springs eternal! God bless and much love.

# Daily Devotions

———◇◇◇———

Good morning! Read Psalm 119:11 and Ephesians 5:17–20. You are what you eat is a well-known cliché that carries a lot of truth. If you want a healthy body, you should have a healthy diet. To become wise, you must gain wisdom. What we allow in our heart and mind becomes who we are. To live a godly life, we must fill our life with godly things that meet God's approval. Ask yourself, is what you're feeding your heart, soul, and mind meeting God's approval? Are you walking in God's ways or your own? God bless and much love.

# Daily Devotions

―――――◇◇◇◇◇◇◇―――――

Good morning! Read Psalm 119:33–40. The more we are taught, the more we learn. However, it's by having the desire to learn that we learn the most. The lack of the desire to learn will minimize what you learn. But having the willingness to learn opens the doors to further learning. It takes a willingness and desire to learn and understand the things of God! As you grow in your knowledge of God, you are also strengthening your relationship with God! As you grow in God's Word, God's Word grows in you! God bless and much love.

# Daily Devotions

Good morning! Read Psalm 37:3–6 and 122:1 and Matthew 7:19–21, then 1 Corinthians 4:18. Where is your favorite place to go where you find peace, contentment, and joy? What's your heart's desire for lasting fulfillment? Is it something that will last or does it have a temporary shelf life? Is your life structured in a way whereas these dreams can and will come true? If not, what can you change about you that will put you on the right path to accomplish what your heart desires? Just a little food for thought! Hint: Try God! God bless and much love.

# Daily Devotions

———◇◇◇◇◇———

Good morning! Read John 8:31–32 and Romans 1:16, then 1 Corinthians 12:4–11. God has given us many gifts. These gifts are not to be kept to ourselves but to be shared to others who are lost and searching for the things that make life complete. The greatest gift that we can share is His Word. It is the power of the gospel that enhances and changes lives. It's the power of the gospel that changed our life! Its truth has set us free and its truth can set anyone free. But it's up to us to share this good news to others that they may be free as well. God bless and much love.

# Daily Devotions

———◇◇◇◇◇———

Good morning! Read Jeremiah 18:1–6. Whenever clay is in the potter's hands, the potter shapes and molds the clay into what he would have it to be. But for this to be done, the clay must be in the potter's hands. God is our Potter, and we are the clay. For God to change our life and reshape it and mold it into something new, we must first place our life in His hands. Only then can the change happen that we desire. Only then can we have a new life with promise. Are you in the Potter's hands? God bless and much love.

# Daily Devotions

———◇◇◇◇———

Good morning! Read 1 John 4:10–19. Everyone has a desire to be loved. Being loved and feeling loved provides a serenity and comfort of its own. It's the love inside us that has a yearning and desire for love. However, it's the perfect love of God that gives us completeness in the love we continually seek. It's not the love we have for God but the love God has for us that is made perfect in us. Having the foundation of the love of God makes us whole and complete! Do you feel God's love? God bless and much love.

# Daily Devotions

Good morning! Read Proverbs 16:18 and Matthew 23:12, then Galatians 1:10. Often many try to impress others by speaking highly of themselves. Exalting themselves to a higher standard of who they really are in an effort to persuade their peers. However, in the eyes of God, it's their humbleness and humility that persuades God to exalt them to a higher standard before Him. It's their pride that lifts them up, and it's their pride that will lead to their fall! Stay humble and let God exalt you in your life! God bless and much love.

# Daily Devotions

---

Good morning! Read Romans 2:21–23 and 14:16. The way we live our lives is an example to our children, family, friends, and acquaintances. It's so important that we are a good example, especially for our children! Children are always watching and listening to what is seen and heard! If we talk the talk, we should walk the walk! Not say one thing and do another but be consistent in what we teach and preach to others! Remember, you're always being observed by someone! Live honestly and truthfully in Christ Jesus! God bless and much love.

# Daily Devotions

———◇◈◇———

Good morning! Read John 15:1–8–16. A tree fuels its branches what it needs to bear fruit. The heart sends the body through the blood what it needs to survive. As the branches are veins to the tree, we are veins to the Body of Christ. To give His body what is needed to bear fruit which is the Word and sayings of God. It is God that cultivates and nourishes the tree, but we must cultivate and nourish our heart to receive the things of God. The branch without the tree cannot survive and neither can we without God. God bless and much love.

# Daily Devotions

———◇◇◇◇———

Good morning! Read Psalm 46:10 and Isaiah 26:3–4. There are times in life when so much is happening we have to take a moment and pause. To take a deep breath and plan our next move. When our life is cluttered with so many things, we have to pause and put things in order. Many miss the beauty of life and life's surroundings because they don't pause and take that moment and deep breath. The child of God can always turn to God and pause and pray, and God will give His peace and provide the proper order that's missing in their life. God bless and much love.

# Daily Devotions

━━━━◇◈◇◈◇━━━━

Good morning! Read Matthew 11:28–30 and Philippians 4:5–7. Whenever many face hardships and problems they will talk to nearly anyone but the *right one*! They will read every self-help book they can find but omit reading the *right book*! The *right one* is Jesus Christ who invites all to come unto Him. To lay their burdens down before Him. The *right book* is the Word of God! It's in His Word that we find the comfort and strength needed to get through the obstacles of this life! God bless and much love.

# Daily Devotions

Good morning! Read Matthew 9:20–22 and 12:10. Having faith is important to the believers of Christ. What's even more important is that we stretch our faith in our praise and prayer to God! Many miracles done by Christ involved prayer and faith and action on the part of the recipient. The woman with the issue of blood stretched out her hand to touch the garment of Jesus as did the man with the withered hand to be healed. They stretched out their hand in faith! Are you stretching out your faith to Christ? God bless and much love.

# Daily Devotions

———————◇◈◇———————

Good morning! Read Luke 6:36–42. With the expanse of television, radio, and social media many are publicly critical and opinionated of their views of other people. From politicians to the pulpit, personal attacks are rampant! Not acknowledging their own faults but pointing out the faults of others. In the eyes of God, we should judge no one! Especially when we have faults of our own. Before you become critical of someone else, make sure your life is straight! Judge not, and you shall not be judged! God bless and much love.

# Daily Devotions

---

Good morning! Read Deuteronomy 30:11–19. Some of the easiest exams to take are open-book exams. What's even easier is when they have the answers to the questions asked. The Bible has all the answers about life's questions pertaining to how to live. They are not hidden nor too far to reach but are always available to all. From blessings and curses to life and death, the Bible has the answers! However, to know and learn the answers to your questions about life, you must first open the book! God bless and much love.

# Daily Devotions

———◇◇◇———

Good morning! Read Matthew 3:16–17 and 4:1–11, then 1 Corinthians 10:13. Everyone who comes to Christ will go through a time of testing. An onslaught of trials and temptations from the wicked one, hitting at your weakest points to destroy the faith you are beginning to build. Although you may fail at times stay strong in faith, trust in God's Word and use God's Word to overcome the various trials you will go through. Christ defeated Satan with the Word of God replying, "It is written" and so can you! God bless and much love.

# Daily Devotions

---

Good morning! Read Job 33:21–30 and Joel 2:25–28. How often have you listened to a song or watched a movie and liked a part or missed a part and hit Rewind to hear it or see it again? How often have you wished you could go back to a time in your life and hit Rewind and do some things differently than you did? To change somethings that would change your life. Only God can renew your life and restore what you've lost and give you a new beginning. But you must call on His name and ask Him to hit Rewind. God bless and much love.

# Daily Devotions

---

Good morning! Read 2 Corinthians 3:5 and Philippians 4:19. Often many work as much as they can to ensure they earn enough to meet their needs. That their bills are paid and that they have enough food to eat and clothes to wear and hopefully having enough left over to save a little for that rainy day. But those who look to God realize that God is our sufficiency in all things. He knows our needs before we have them and will provide a way according to His riches in glory by Christ Jesus! God bless and much love.

# Daily Devotions

———⬦⬦⬦⬦⬦———

Good morning! Read Matthew 4:4 and Romans 1:16. The written Word of God is the spoken Word of God and the spoken Word of God is the written Word of God! It's more than just a verse here or a chapter there! It's a complete love letter from our God to us. Only by understanding the entire Word of God do we fully understand God! The reasons for the punishments and the reasons for the blessings. We only understand a puzzle when the pieces are in place, and we only understand God by knowing His Word! God bless and much love.

# Daily Devotions

———◇◇◈◇◇———

Good morning! Read Luke 6:46–49 and John 14:23–24. As children, our parents taught us, and we believed because we loved them. God is our Father and is teaching us how to live a life with His blessings that we may live a peaceful and joyful life. We believed our parents as children because we loved them! Should we not also believe God if we love Him? Too often we question God with skepticism and doubt! But you shouldn't put a question mark where God has put a period! Listen, learn, believe, and grow! God bless and much love.

# Daily Devotions

---

G ood morning! Read Romans 6:3–10 and Galatians 2:20. When you are in Christ, you have died to yourself so you may have a new life in Him. Yet it's not you who lives, but it's Christ who's living in you! Being spiritually buried with Christ in the baptism of the heart, you are spiritually resurrected to a new and rewarding life! To living a life that is Christ centered in all things you say and do! Having the shackles of sin removed that you may live freely in Christ unto God! Be free! Live free! Be blessed in Christ! God bless and much love.

# Daily Devotions

---

Good morning! Read Deuteronomy 30:11–19. Everything we buy comes with instructions. There's a how-to for our health, food preparation, our car, and everything that needs to be assembled. God has given us a how-to book on how to live. It contains everything we need to live a life full of God's blessings. It also warns us of what the results are if we don't. The price we pay for His word is freely given. It's up to us to follow the instructions. God's instructions are not burdensome but frees us from the burdens of life. God bless and much love.

# Daily Devotions

———◇◇◇◇◇———

Good morning! Read Jeremiah 9:23–24 and 1 Corinthians 1:23–31. There are many in society who may be considered intellectual giants because of their intelligence in certain areas. Yet their intellect is foolishness when compared to that of God. God has taken what they consider foolish to confound the wise and the weak things of the world to confound the things which are mighty. The greatest glory is not in our natural intellect but in our understanding of knowing the righteousness of God! God bless and much love.

# Daily Devotions

---◈◈◈◈◈---

Good morning! Read John 10:10. The movie *Silence of the Lambs* is a well-known movie. The devil is on a mission to silence the lambs of God! To silence the voices of the children of God from speaking the wonderful works of God! The devil attempts to silence us through unexpected health issues, unexpected financial issues, and division of the unity of Christ. All these are to create doubt. These temporary setbacks are a setup for God to do something greater in our life! Keep trusting in God! God bless and much love.

# Daily Devotions

———◇◇◇◇◇———

Good morning! Read Jeremiah 9:23–24 and 2 Timothy 2:15. To get to know someone, you must take the time to get to know them. Otherwise, they are just an acquaintance or someone you know of but don't really know them for who they are. Every believer in God must take the time to know God, or God is just an acquaintance or someone you know of but don't really know Him or who He really is or what He's about. Have you taken the time to get to know Him? Do you study and believe His Word? God bless and much love.

# Daily Devotions

———◇◈◇◈◇———

Good morning! Read Matthew 15:16–20 and Ephesians 4:29–32. We use filters for many things. From oil filters and fuel filters in our cars to filters in swimming pools to remove debris and deposits that can be harmful to their performance. Just as we use filters in other things, we should also filter what enters our heart and mind. To filter out and remove what can be harmful to us and harmful and offensive to others. That our communication and relationships with others may be kind and uplifting and edifying! God bless and much love.

# Daily Devotions

―――――◇◇◇◇◇◇―――――

Good morning! Read Acts 17:10–11 and 20:28, then 2 Timothy 2:15 and 2 Peter 1:20–21. We like confirmation when we buy something. Some form of receipt of proof of what was purchased. When we hear the Word of God taught or preached, we should also go to His word to confirm what we heard is truly God's word and not someone's opinion or interpretation. We were purchased with the blood of Christ and confirmation is our obedience to God. God's Word is itemized in detail. It details proof of purchase. God bless and much love.

# Daily Devotions

---

Good morning! Read Deuteronomy 31:6 and Joshua 1:7–9. Having the favor of God is having the power of God in every challenge we face. Walking in the power of faith in all we do. Observing to do all that God says. Not turning to the right or left because of fear but having the strength of God and courage to prosper in all we do. Doing all things in the name of God and giving God thanks in all things. Understanding and knowing it is God that causes us to overcome in everything that His Word and name be glorified. God bless and much love.

# Daily Devotions

---

Good morning! Read 2 Corinthians 13:5–8. Whether at work or school, there is usually a periodic evaluation. At work, an evaluation is done of our work performance. At school, our grades indicate how well we are doing. But how often do we evaluate ourselves? Are you living as you should? Are you treating others with the love and respect like you want to be treated? If you believe in God, are you living in the faith of Jesus Christ? It's time to examine and evaluate yourself? Will you pass? God bless and much love.

# Daily Devotions

---

Good morning! Read Joshua 1:5–9. There are many who read self-help books or talk to professionals to gain confidence and rid themselves of the fears they may have. It could be stress or anxiety or fear itself, but all want to live a life that is calm. Living with God as the center of your life, you'll find strength and courage that overcomes your fears. God doesn't want us to have any fears but to live a life with confidence and faith in Him. This begins with first believing and having trust in Him! God bless and much love.

# Daily Devotions

---

Good morning! Read 2 Samuel 22:2–7. We face many challenges in life. Some can be so overwhelming we at times say, "What's the use in trying." During these times is when we need to call on God who can overwhelm what overwhelms us. Praising God *before* these trials occur will lessen their impact when they do occur. We like to be in good standing with our family and friends. We're in good standing with God by our trust and faith in Him. Your confidence in God assures you of His power to deliver you. God bless and much love.

# Daily Devotions

---

Good morning! Read Acts 5:42 and Colossians 2:16–19. There has been much debate concerning the Sabbath Day for many years. Some say Saturday and others say Sunday. Only to become a judge of one another causing division among the people of God. Being a child of God means every day is treated as a Sabbath and Holy Day. Daily we are to teach and preach Christ Jesus and not judge anyone who believes in respect of a Holy Day. These are merely a shadow of things to come; but the body is of Christ. God bless and much love.

# Daily Devotions

---

Good morning! Read Proverbs 16:9 and 2 Thessalonians 3:5. There are several directions to any place we desire to go. Some take the long way, and some prefer a more direct way to go. The one place every Christian desires to go is where eternity is spent in the presence of God. Only God can guide us and give us the right direction and road in life to Him. The Holy Spirit will direct our hearts into the love of God, and into the patient waiting for Christ. But you must follow the right direction! Are you? God bless and much love.

# Daily Devotions

———◇———

Good morning! Read Psalm 121:1–8 and Hebrews 4:16. Whether you are rich or poor, we all go through seasons of uncertainty. We look for guidance and helpful advice for clarity of what may be troubling in our life. The child of God will lift up their eyes unto the hills, from whence cometh their help. Our help comes from God! God will always keep His children on the right path when we look to Him for direction. It's by going to His throne of grace that we find help in our time of need! God bless and much love.

# Daily Devotions

ood morning! Read Titus 2:11–15. It's by the grace of God that the salvation of God is made available to all. We are taught and learn to refuse all ungodliness and worldly lust and how to live soberly, righteously and godly, in this present world. Preparing ourselves and staying prepared for the return of Christ Jesus who gave Himself for us to redeem us from all sin and to purify us from the bondage of ungodliness and worldly lust! Always being thankful to God for His amazing grace that has saved us! God bless and much love.

# Daily Devotions

Good morning! Read Isaiah 45:18–19 and John 23–24, then Ephesians 1:3–5. When we strive for anything, we have a purpose in mind. When God created the heavens and the earth, God had a purpose in His mind. It's not that God was lonely because all things were in Him before creation. Because of His great love we are here to share and be a part of who He is. Finding our purpose can only be found when we go to the main source which is God. Only by submitting to Him can we find our planned purpose in life. God bless and much love.

# Daily Devotions

---

G ood morning! Read Luke 4:1–13 and James 4:7–10. As we pursue the goodness and righteousness of God, we must recognize that the devil is also pursuing after us. To distract us with false and temporary pleasures in his efforts to turn us to the right or left from the path that leads to God. It's so important that we remain focused in our heart and mind on God's Word to overcome what the devil lays in our path. As we draw closer to God, God draws closer to us. Having power in the name of Jesus Christ that causes the devil to flee. God bless and much love.

# Daily Devotions

---

Good morning! Read Galatians 1:6–10 and 6:7. Every child of God seeks the truth in the Word of God. Unfortunately, there are some who will alter God's Word to fit their selfish agenda to attract a following for themselves. In effect, bringing God down to their level instead of rising to the level of God. Leading those seeking away from the truth they so much desire to have. Not considering the judgment of God but setting out to receive praise for themselves. By knowing His Word for yourself, you will not be lead astray! God bless and much love.

# Daily Devotions

---

G ood morning! Luke 5:36–39 and 2 Corinthians 5:17. No one buys a new car and has the old parts from their old car put in the new car. They understand that for a new car to function like a new car, it must be equipped with new parts. This same thought must apply to living a new life in Christ! You must fully get rid of the old you to fully embrace the new you to fully grow in Christ Jesus! Old baggage weighs down any new relationship, and old baggage can weigh down a new relationship with Christ Jesus! God bless and much love.

# Daily Devotions

———◇◇◇◇◇———

Good morning! Read Galatians 5:22–26. A healthy diet results in you having a healthy body. Proper exercise helps strengthen your body. A healthy and strong body gives you confidence mentally in having a positive attitude about life. It's also important that we feed our spirit a healthy diet of spiritual things such as the Word of God! It's by strengthening our spirit in God's Word that we are made stronger in faith in the things of God! Being strong in spirit increases your spiritual mindset in living a spiritual life! God bless and much love.

# Daily Devotions

G ood morning! Read Proverbs 16:9 and 2 Corinthians 8:12–15 and 9:7. The mind is as strong as the heart, and the heart is rooted by what's in the mind. Both work together to establish who we are. Like one hand washing the other, the heart and mind must work together. The children of God represent the heart and mind of God. To love and care for one another that no one lacks but are equal in all things. Giving to others as our God has given to us. We do this not grudgingly but with joy in our heart. God bless and much love.

# Daily Devotions

***

G ood morning! Read Leviticus 20:26 and John 14:23–24 and 15:16. God is Holy and has called and separated His chosen from the world that we may be Holy. Being obedient to what God says is evidence of our desire to be Holy to which we have been called. To strive for the perfection that God continuously perfects in us daily. Putting aside the weakness of the flesh and finding strength in the Spirit to attain the blessings only a Holy God can give. Being thankful and giving thanks in all things. God bless and much love.

# Daily Devotions

---

Good morning! Read 1 Corinthians 13:1–7. It's often said that charity begins at home and home is where the heart is! This charity is the love that springs forth from the heart. Whatever we say or do, if the love isn't in it, it is meaningless and more of just going through the motions. Although we may have faith and hope, without love from the heart, our efforts are futile to say the least. True love enhances our faith and hope and isn't wearied but endures all things. It's the love of God that ignites the love in us! God bless and much love.

# Daily Devotions

———◇◈◇◈◇———

Good morning! Read Romans 8:1–2 and Revelation 21:23–25. When we walk in the Spirit of God and live in the Spirit of God, we are no longer condemned as those (of which we also once were) who live in the flesh apart from God. But the Light of God shines continuously in our lives. There is no darkness in God but only light! Although the darkness of sin may surround us, we no longer willingly serve the darkness of sin. If we fall, the mercy of God forgives us, and the grace of God sustains us! God bless and much love.

# Daily Devotions

---

Good morning! Read 2 Corinthians 11:13–15 and 1 Peter 5:8. The devil is very real and his mission to deceive and destroy as many people as he can is also very real! The devil will use anyone or anything to create havoc and disunity among all people! Transforming himself into "an angel of light" to fool and deceive the masses! But those who know God can unmask the devil through knowledge of the Word of God! The devil poisons lives, and God's Word is the antidote to his poisonous ways! God bless and much love.

# Daily Devotions

———◆◇◆———

Good morning! Read Proverbs 24:29 and Luke 6:27–36, then Romans 12:17–21. To who or whom does vengeance belong? Many times we want to take it upon ourselves to repay someone who has wronged us. The Word of God teaches us just the opposite. We are to forgive and love our enemies. To be able to do this is a blessing within itself. To turn the other cheek shows strength and character. God can repay far better than we can. Don't sink as low as your adversary but rise to the level God has raised you to. God bless and much love.

# Daily Devotions

---⬦⬦⬦---

Good morning! Read Genesis 39:1–3 and 20–23 and John 16:33, then Romans 8:28. When we seek God, we find favor with God. It doesn't make any difference what the world may send your way, having favor with God will cause you to triumph in any and all situations. We overcome by our faith in God who controls all things. It's the Spirit of God that equips us and leads us. The life of Joseph is a great example of God's favor on him. The favor of God led him from prison to governor of the land. His favorable hand has not weakened! You only have to trust Him in every situation. God bless and much love.

# Daily Devotions

———◇◇◇———

Good morning! Read John 9:5 and 11:9–10. When we walk into a room, we can see everything in the room. However, when the room is dark, we can't see anything, yet we know it is furnished. It is only by having light in the room that we see all. Our spiritual lives in God enable us to see all. But without having the Spirit of God, we are no better living than that darkened room. When we have Christ, we have the light! Without Christ, we are blinded by the darkness and must feel our way through life. Does His light shine in you? God bless and much love.

# Daily Devotions

---◇◇◇◇◇---

Good morning! Read John 15:1–10. To have a strong relationship there must be fellowship with one another. Spending time with one another is what strengthens the relationship. Our relationship with God is no different! We must spend time in fellowship with God to strengthen our relationship with God. As in any relationship, there must be agreement for the relationship to grow. Our agreement to God is through our faith and obedience to God. Is your relationship with God growing? God bless and much love.

# Daily Devotions

———◇◇◇◇◇———

G ood morning! Read Deuteronomy 29:29 and 2 Peter 3:17–18. The secret things of God belong to God! However, God reveals many things to us according to our spiritual maturity and growth! It's important that we are not led astray or get sidetracked by the things of the world but remain steadfast in the calling of God for us. That we may grow in grace, and in the knowledge of our Lord and Savior Jesus Christ! We may never know all there is, but knowing something is far better than knowing nothing at all! God bless and much love.

# Daily Devotions

―――――◇◈◇◈◇―――――

Good morning! Read Mark 12:29–31 and 1 John 4:19. To have an intimate relationship with someone, you must have trust. Without trust, you cannot truly have an intimate relationship. God wants to have such a relationship with us. Building any relationship takes time. Our trust builds the more we get to know them. Putting all things aside to get to know the one we love. Making them first place in our life. Putting our heart, soul, mind, and strength in their hands because of the love and trust we have in them. God bless and much love.

# Daily Devotions

Good morning! Read Matthew 12:46–50 and John 17:14–20, then 1 Corinthians 7:19. Family is important. Jesus made a distinct difference between our earthly family and the family of God. God, who is no respecter of persons, accepts all who do His will as His children. Separating His children from the children of the world by His Word. It doesn't matter what color you are or how old you may be. If you accept Him and do His will, you are His. Obeying the will of God and not what we may think or feel is what matters. God bless and much love.

# Daily Devotions

---

Good morning! Read Numbers 32:23 and 2 Chronicles 16:9, then Hebrews 10:26–31. Whenever an agreement is made, there are terms to the agreement. Whether it's insurance, a loan, or anything that is agreed to, there are terms. If the terms are broken, the agreement becomes void. Being in alignment with the will of God are terms of the agreement with God. To willfully be disobedient to God is a violation of what you've agreed to with God. However, His mercy and grace keep the agreement enforced! God bless and much love.

# Daily Devotions

———◆◆◆———

Good morning! Read Ephesians 6:10–17. Every carpenter, mechanic, or builder of any kind has a toolbox with the necessary tools to do their job. Every doctor, lawyer, or teacher has to be well trained to be successful in their profession. Everyone in the military must be prepared for warfare in the event of war. We also must be prepared for the spiritual warfare we face daily! As in every profession preparation is needed, we also must be prepared and stay prepared to battle the evil that besets us daily! God bless and much love.

# Daily Devotions

———◈◈◈———

Good morning! Read Matthew 24:23–27 and John 15:1–8. It has been said, "You can't see the forest because of the trees." More importantly, for many, they can't see *the tree* because of the forest! I'm speaking of the Tree of Life of God that gives life to all who find it. However, there are false trees within the forest of life to deceive many from the true Tree of Life! Jesus Christ is the true vine that gives us the spiritual nourishment needed to live a spiritual life! Have you found Him? God bless and much love.

# Daily Devotions

---◇◇◇◇◇---

Good morning! Read Numbers 13:25–33 and 14:30–34, then 2 Kings 6:15–18. Often decisions are made by the majority! However, at times the majority is not always right! When Moses sent men to spy out the land, two believed God and ten brought words of discouragement and fear! God's truth supersedes the majority! When Elisha was surrounded by his enemies, he believed God, knowing his enemies were surrounded by God and the chariots of fire from God were around him! God *is* the majority! God bless and much love.

# Daily Devotions

---

Good morning! Read Isaiah 55:6–13. Every ladder has limits. It has a certain width and height. Climbing the ladder of success also has limits. You can only go as high as the ladder. Hurting others along the way, with regret, to achieve their goals. Many taking credit for what they've done themselves to get there. Climbing the spiritual ladder of God has no limits. Its width and height are endless. You can go as high as your faith will take you. Having strength to make the right decisions without regret. God bless and much love.

# Daily Devotions

---✦◇✦◇✦---

Good morning! Read Matthew 18:21–35. There are times when we have wronged someone, whether intentional or unintentional, and we ask their forgiveness and they forgave us for what we have done. But there are many who will not forgive others who have done them wrong. Forgiving not only sets the other person free from carrying the burden of guilt and shame, but it set us free as well. Unforgiveness is a chain that is carried until we free ourselves by forgiving. Do you forgive others as you have been forgiven? Or are you still chained by unforgiveness? God bless and much love.

# Daily Devotions

———✦———

Good morning! Read Luke 12:8–12 and Romans 1:16, then 1 Peter 3:15–17. Every follower of Christ has been asked or will be asked the reason for their belief. We are never to sheepishly shy away but are to be bold and confident in our answers to all who question our faith. Knowing that denying Him, we are also denied by Him! Therefore, we look to God who will give us the words needed that those hearing and questioning will be saved just as we have been saved. Every day is the day of salvation for someone! God bless and much love.

# Daily Devotions

---

Good morning! Read Luke 16:10–12. As we grow from childhood to adulthood, we learn many things along the way. Our education in school and learning the different things in life help to shape and mold us into the person we are today. We are not given everything at once but given as much as we are able to handle. As we grow and mature in Christ, we are educated by the Word of God, and our faith is shaped and molded by the Holy Spirit. During this growth, we are given as much as we can handle. Are you growing? God bless and much love.

# Daily Devotions

---

Good morning! Read Matthew 18:22–35. There are times we seek forgiveness and mercy from others for our offenses we have done to them. Yet there are some who are unforgiving and harsh to others for lesser offenses they have done to them even though they themselves have been forgiven and shown mercy for their greater offense. This behavior is not only seen in the eyes of God but is also witnessed by those they know. To receive forgiveness from God you must be completely forgiving yourself! God bless and much love.

# Daily Devotions

———◈◈◈◈◈———

Good morning! Read Psalm 116:1–9. God is always open and attentive to the prayers of His children. Our concerns are God's concerns! Understanding God is our deliverer in all things! It's God who makes our crooked path straight and makes a way when there seems to be no way. To deliver us from the seemingly impossible task before us! Wherever we go, God goes before us to prepare the way for us! That we may walk before the Lord in the land of the living! Being sustained by His mercy and grace! God bless and much love.

# Daily Devotions

———◇◇◇◇◇———

Good morning! Read Matthew 19:4–6 and 1 Corinthians 6:17–20, then 2 Timothy 3:16–17. When two are joined together in marriage, they are no longer two but are now one flesh. Not to be separated by anyone. When we are joined to God, we are now one spirit with Him, not to be separated by anyone. It is the devil's desire to separate both. To come between you and God. To weaken you through doubt and unbelief. Stay strong in the righteousness of God, knowing God is complete in us as He makes us complete in Him. God bless and much love.

# Daily Devotions

———◆◇◆———

Good morning! Read Isaiah 41:10 and 2 Timothy 1:7. One of the most powerful weapons that the devil uses is that of fear. But God says to us, "Fear not!" The words "fear not" appear in the Bible 365 times. One for each day. God is with us in everything that we go through when we rely on Him and look to Him for deliverance, healing, or overcoming any obstacle that confronts us. It's God who leads us and strengthens to overcome. And we overcome fear by our faith in the finished works of Jesus Christ. God bless and much love.

# Daily Devotions

---

Good morning! Read Proverbs 3:1–8. Every student must pay attention to learn the subject matter that is being taught. Every new worker must pay attention to learn their new job. Every patient with an ailment must follow the doctor's instructions to be relieved of their health problem. Following what is taught or the instructions given is how we progress. God has given instructions on how to live this life. Just as we trust our teachers and doctors, we must trust God who has given us this life! Do you trust God? God bless and much love.

# Daily Devotions

———◆———

Good morning! Read John 20:29 and 1 Peter 1:6–9. For many, it's seeing is believing! But for the child of God, we believe in God whom we have not seen. We believe because we have seen His working power working in our lives. We believe because we have seen God make our crooked lives straight. We believe because we have seen and felt His great love He has for those we do believe. It's when we believe that we see and recognize the fullness of what God can and will do in our lives! God bless and much love.

# Daily Devotions

---

Good morning! Read Ecclesiastes 8:16 and James 1:5–8. We do better at things when our heart is in it. Otherwise, we're just going through the motions. When we apply our heart to having godly wisdom, our relationship with God is strengthened! When we assemble in church to worship God, if our heart isn't in it, we're just assembling together in church. It's by having a desire in applying our heart to God that grants us the godly wisdom our heart longs to have. This desire is done in faith! God bless and much love.

# Daily Devotions

---

Good morning! Read Jeremiah 29:11–13. As we look back on our years of life, we see and remember our successes and our failures. For some, the past has given them hope for the future, and for others, their hopes may be diminished. However, we must remember, as long as we are alive, God is our hope and salvation in our days ahead! God's plan for you is still actively working in your life! Therefore, trust and believe and have faith in God's plan for you! Turn to God for renewed hope! Allow God to work in you! God bless and much love.

# Daily Devotions

———◇∞◇∞◇———

Good morning! Read Luke 23:46 and John 16:13–15, then Romans 10:9–13. Being born again, believing in God and the resurrection of Jesus Christ, we are saved. Receiving the Holy Spirit of God, we in turn commend this Spirit to God for our learning and direction to live a life pleasing to God. Repenting and dying of ourselves and living a new life in Christ Jesus. Being sanctified by God, to God, for the purpose of God, fulfilling His will that we may prosper in all things. Not just knowing of Christ but believing in Christ. God bless and much love.

# Daily Devotions

———✧✧✧———

Good morning! Read Isaiah 59:1 and John 1:1–4, then Romans 10:9–11. Everything has a beginning and a starting point. Everything except God, who has no beginning and no end, for He is the creator of all things. God is always ready to give anyone a new beginning and a new start. It doesn't matter how young or old you are, God is ready with an open ear and a stretched-out hand to save all who are lost and need a new lease on life. To be reborn and filled with the Spirit of God can change your life and give you that new start. God bless and much love.

# Daily Devotions

---

Good morning! Read Mark 16:15–20 and John 14:12, then Philippians 2:5. The last commandment Jesus Christ gave was that we should go and preach the gospel throughout the world that all may have an opportunity to hear the Gospel. We were also given authority to do the works of Christ in His name. It should be also understood that all we do in the name of Christ will be confirmed by signs and wonders to follow. We are the representatives of Christ! Let us live and walk accordingly! God bless and much love.

# Daily Devotions

———※———

Good morning! Read Luke 9:1–6 and John 14:12. When Jesus sent forth His disciples, He gave them authority to do many things. This same authority we have today when we believe and accept Christ as our Savior. What's most important is that we *believe*! When we believe in the authority we have been given, we can accomplish more in whatever task we undertake. However, it must be understood that our will must be in alignment with the will of God. With God, nothing is impossible! God bless and much love.

# Daily Devotions

———❖❖———

Good morning! Read Deuteronomy 31:8. God will never leave us nor forsake us! It's God that goes before us to direct our way. It's important to know and understand that God will go before us, but He *will not* go for us! We must take the necessary steps following His direction! When we get off track or offline with God, God is still on track and online with us! God's promise is to never leave us nor forsake us! It's important that we never leave nor forsake Him! Without God, we are lost! God bless and much love.

# Daily Devotions

---

Good morning! Read Romans 7:15–25. Often many set goals and make plans with sincere intentions to meet those goals and fulfill their intentions. They have the will to do something but lack the commitment to get it done! Some are committed but lack the willpower to get started! What they want to do, they don't do, and what they don't want to do, they do! It's the war within that's become the stumbling block! The spirit is willing, but the flesh is weak! However, a strong spirit will upgrade the weakness of the flesh! God bless and much love.

# Daily Devotions

---

Good morning! Read Luke 17:11–19. Whenever a crisis arises, many will look to God for help. Whether it's healing from a sickness or restored health in another area or a financial problem or relationship problems or something in other areas that need God's deliverance. Sadly, when God has saved and delivered, many forget about God and resume living an ungodly life. Understand, this hypocritical style of living is not pleasing to God! Give God continuous praise for all He has done for you in your life! God bless and much love.

# Daily Devotions

---

Good morning! Read Hebrews 4:9–11. We always feel better after a good night's rest. Our body feels good, and our mind is alert and clear. When we are rested, we are able to go about our day on a positive note. Having a strong belief in God gives rest to our soul and spirit. When our soul and spirit are at rest, we are able to find comfort in God through the various conditions of life. It's this rest in God that we labor to work for! Just as we love our rest on a rainy night, we can rest peacefully during the storms of life! God bless and much love.

# Daily Devotions

———◇◇◇◇———

Good morning! Read Jeremiah 17:5–10 and John 15:1–7. When a tree is planted in good soil and watered, the tree will grow and bear good fruit. If the tree is not watered and uprooted, the tree will die. When we are planted and watered in the Word of God, we too will grow and bear fruit. If we are uprooted from His Word, we also will cease to bear the fruit of His blessings and will die a spiritual death. Having our trust, faith, and hope in God will enhance every area of our life. Without these three is the same as that uprooted tree! God bless and much love.

# Daily Devotions

———⬧⬧⬧———

Good morning! Read Luke 9:23–26 and John 5:21–24. There are many on a mission of the pursuit of happiness! But what type of happiness are they pursuing? Is it materialistic luxuries or peace of mind? Is it something that is lasting or temporary fulfillment? The most important question is, do you lose sight of yourself in the process? It's through Jesus Christ that we lose ourself to find ourself. Taking up His cross daily in pursuit of true happiness that leads to the treasures only God can give. But to deny Christ is to deny God. God bless and much love.

# Daily Devotions

---

Good morning! Read Deuteronomy 8:17–18 and Proverbs 8:17–21, then Philippians 4:11–13 and 1 Timothy 6:10–12. In the world, money is power and power is money. The pursuit of money has caused many to error from the faith. Seeking wealth without fully being satisfied. Not realizing that all power and wealth is of God. God has made provision for us with the finished works of Christ and has instructed us to be content with what we have. What God gives is of more value than materialistic wealth that you cannot take with you when you leave this life. Seek God's treasure. God bless and much love.

# Daily Devotions

———◇◆◇◆◇———

Good morning! Read Luke 8:5–15. Nearly everyone has an opportunity to hear and receive the Word of God. However, many cannot receive the Word of a God for various reasons. Some are hindered by material things and the lust for riches, and others succumb to peer pressure in maintaining a certain image. But those who receive God's Word have prepared their heart and mind with sincerity to keep God's Word! To dig deeper into the mysteries of the kingdom of God and to draw closer to His heart! God bless and much love.

# Daily Devotions

G ood morning! Read Ephesians 4:4–7 and 11–15. There are many different beliefs, and because of so much confusion, there are different beliefs within those beliefs. But the true child of God believes there is only one Lord, one faith, one baptism! We live by the faith of Jesus Christ and have the measure of grace as a gift of God! Doing our best to edify and build the Body of Christ. Many of us have different roles but the same purpose in this life! To speak the truth of God in Christ working in us! God bless and much love.

# Daily Devotions

———✦✧✦———

Good morning! Read Romans 5:1–5 and James 1:2–4 and 12–15. Our relationship with God is strengthened by our faith. However, the devil will test and try your faith in an attempt to hinder and weaken your relationship with God. But it's maintaining our faith through these various trials that we learn patience and perseverance. By overcoming by our faith is our faith strengthened, and our relationship with God is stronger! It's by enduring through these trials that we are blessed by God! God bless and much love.

# Daily Devotions

---

Good morning! Read Daniel 12:1–3 and 1 Thessalonians 4:12–18, then Revelation 20:12–15. Whenever there's a tryout for a team, every athlete practices to be better skilled in preparation for the tryouts so their chances are better to make the team. Every student studies to prepare to pass their exam. It's how we prepare beforehand that gives us success. In this life, we prepare for the judgment of God at the appointed Judgment Day. Are you preparing yourself the make His team? Team Jesus! God bless and much love.

# Daily Devotions

———✦———

Good morning! Read Psalm 95:7–11 and 138:2–4. When someone is at a distance, it's difficult to hear their voice when they're trying to speak to you. Trying to filter out the sounds around you is made easier when you get closer to the person speaking to you. If you know the voice, its sound stands out from other sounds and voices. The voice of God is heard through His Word. God is so strong concerning His Word, He has magnified His Word above His name. The more you know His Word, the clearer you hear His voice. Are you close enough? Do you hear His voice? God bless and much love.

# Daily Devotions

---

Good morning! Read 1 Timothy 4:1–2 and James 2:19, then 1 John 4:1. Everyone desires to have the real thing. To find the truth about something and not a cheap imitation. To know the facts! The truth is facts can change but the truth never does. An ice cube is a fact, but the truth is, it is water. God's Word is truth! The devil tries to water down God's Word, but even the devil trembles at the truth of God. Using his spirit to deceive many with cheap imitations to destroy the lives of those seeking the truth of God. Beware! God bless and much love.

# Daily Devotions

G ood morning! Read Isaiah 40:3–8 and Matthew 24:34–36, then John 1:23. Isaiah wrote of "the voice crying in the wilderness" to "make straight the way of the Lord!" He was speaking of John the Baptist who prepared the way for the coming of Christ. Today, as children of God, we are the voices crying in the wilderness making straight the way for the return of Christ! Not just preparing ourselves but preaching and teaching others that they may be prepared as well! Only God knows the day, and *that day* will come! God bless and much love.

# Daily Devotions

---

Good morning! Read Psalm 26:1–12. When a student has diligently prepared for an exam, they are anxious to take the exam. They are confident in their preparation with budding excitement feeling confident they will pass the exam. The child of God should have this same confidence in their walk with God! That we may be judged and examined by God having assurance and confidence we will pass His exam of our spiritual walk in life with Him. Are you prepared to be judged and examined by God? God bless and much love.

# Daily Devotions

———◇◇◇◇◇———

Good morning! Read Romans 10:9–13 and Hebrews 11:1 and 6. Everything that has an end has a beginning, and nothing is finished unless it's first started. Our decision to stand for God begins with accepting God and Jesus Christ as our Savior. The longer we stand the more we believe and the more we believe the stronger our faith grows. Through our faith we always have hope. Our hope relies on our continued trust in God. These steps will carry you from the beginning of your stand for God to the end! God bless and much love.

# Daily Devotions

---❊❊❊---

Good morning! Read Philippians 4:11–13 and 19. Growing in the Word of God is a learning process. Just as climbing a mountain, the more you climb, the closer you get to the top. The higher you climb, the better the view and the more you are able to see what's around you. Our understanding and knowledge grows as we grow, and our ability increases because as we grow our faith grows. That faith is in Christ! It's through Him that we are able to do what we do! It's Christ who gives us strength! God bless and much love.

# Daily Devotions

---

Good morning! Read Isaiah 6:8 and Luke 9:1–6, then John 13:20. God sent prophets to the people to speak His word just as Christ sent His disciples to not only to preach the kingdom of God but gave them authority and power to do so. What was given then still applies to us today. When our testimony and message is received, in truth, they are receiving the Spirit of God in Christ being revealed through us. That our thoughts may be His thoughts and our words may be His words. Being as sheep who only hear their Shepherd's voice. God bless and much love.

# Daily Devotions

Good morning! Read Matthew 12:25–30 and 1 Corinthians 1:10–18. Every coach encourages their players to play and compete as one. As a team being one unit playing as one. No one player is above the team, but every player is a big part of the team. Each player has a role to play. Any team divided cannot be a winning team if the players don't work together. The same applies to us in our walk in Christ Jesus. As teammates, we can only be winners by supporting and encouraging one another. Christ is not divided but is One. God bless and much love.

# Daily Devotions

---

Good morning! Read Romans 5:19–21 and 2 Corinthians 10:3–6, then Ephesians 6:10–18. There is an ongoing battle between the flesh and the spirit. A battle within the imagination of the mind! It's extremely important that you cast down the ungodly and sinful thoughts that may attempt to enter your thoughts and bring them into captivity by your obedience of Christ! Having on the helmet of salvation and the armor of God to resist all sinful influences with the strength of the Word of God! God bless and much love.

# Daily Devotions

---

Good morning! Read Psalm 90:4–6 and 12. Only God knows the number of the days of life for each of us. We know our beginning of life, but only God knows the number of days we will live on this earth. For this reason, it's important that we make every day count! That we take no day for granted but live and walk in wisdom to live each day to the fullest. It's what we do in this life that prepares us for the afterlife. Whether it's in the kingdom of heaven with God or the kingdom of darkness without God! God bless and much love.

# Daily Devotions

---

Good morning! Read Matthew 6:19–21. Many invest in the stock market, mutual funds, savings accounts, real estate, etc., to receive a return on their investment. There is always some risk involved when they do. A down market, low interest rates, identify theft, foreclosure, etc., which can be a risk to any investor. However, when we invest in God, it's a no risk factor! It cannot be stolen nor lose its value. Our heart is our greatest treasure! When we give our heart to God, we are guaranteed the highest return! God bless and much love.

# Daily Devotions

---

Good morning! Read Joshua 14:9–11. When we commit to the obedience of God, God is faithful in His commitment to us. Our prime years of life are lengthened whereas no matter how old we get, having the favor of God with us, we remain in our prime. Our example of our obedience is an example for our children to follow so the blessings that God has bestowed on us will follow them as well. It's through our obedience that our children learn obedience. It's not just about us; it's also about our children! God bless and much love.

# Daily Devotions

———— ◈◈◈ ————

Good morning! Read Matthew 5:13–16 and 2 Timothy 1:8–13. Those who God has called were called with a holy calling according to His purpose and grace in Christ Jesus before the world began. The Holy Spirit being revealed in you as a light that shines reflecting the glory of God. Not being ashamed but living a life with boldness and praise to God. Even in a room filled with unbelievers we can stand, even if alone, professing our faith of the One who is faithful. Being steadfast in His doctrine of faith and love in Christ Jesus. God bless and much love.

# Daily Devotions

———◆◆◆◆———

Good morning! Read Matthew 24:9–14 and 1 Corinthians 9:24–27. It takes physical endurance to enable us to make it to the end of a race, season, etc. Without the proper physical conditioning, we struggle to the end. Living a spiritual life unto God can also be a struggle. A struggle against the things not of God to hold us back from doing the things of God! This takes spiritual endurance to finish this race in life! It's a race we must endure until to end to receive the prize from God that awaits us! God bless and much love.

# Daily Devotions

---

Good morning! Read Job 23:11–13 and Psalm 119:103–105, then Jeremiah 15:16. Everyone has certain cravings from time to time. A need and desire for certain taste or smell or touch. When we are filled with the Spirit of God, our spirit in us has a constant craving and yearning for His Spirit. It's this Spirit that gives us a desire and leads us to His Word. It's His Word that is the light that guides our path. Like a child yearns to be held by its mother, we yearn to be held by the Spirit of God! God bless and much love.

# Daily Devotions

---

Good morning! Read Ezekiel 14:6 and 36:25–28. Many times we are sorry and apologize for the wrongs we have done. We tell ourselves and those we have harmed we will never do those same things again. However, unless we repent (having a change of mind and heart) those same things are waiting to happen again. Only God can give us real change in our lives. Only God can bring us from the outhouse of this life to the penthouse of life in Christ! But you must repent first! God bless and much love.

# Daily Devotions

———◈◈◈———

Good morning! Read Daniel 10:12–13 and 1 Thessalonians 2:18, then 1 John 4:4 and Revelation 12:7–13. God has blessed and continually sends His blessings to us. God's Angels are also among us to lead us and fight the devil's attempt to block and hold back the blessings and purpose God has for us. The Spirit of God in us is greater than anything that the devil may send our way to allow us to receive what God has meant for us. "What God has blessed shall be blessed!" Only our lack of faith will keep the blessings of God from us. God bless and much love.

# Daily Devotions

---

Good morning! Read Mark 11:12–14 and 20–24. There is power in the Word of God and that power is released when spoken. God's power will enable you to overcome all circumstances when His word is spoken. Whether for healing over sickness and disease or any burden that you have, speaking the promises of His Word releases the power of His Word. A car only moves when you put the pedal to the metal. If not, you just sit there idling. To walk, you must move your feet. If not, you go nowhere. All spoken is done in faith! God bless and much love.

# Daily Devotions

---

Good morning! Read John 15:7–11. When we strive to do the will of God, we can live a life with expectation. Having the expectation of God by being faithful to His Word when we show our confidence and faith in Him. We can expect deliverance in our times of struggle and healing from all sickness and disease. However, we must understand it's according to God's plan for us. It's according to His timing in our life and not ours. We are to live our life with expectation by standing on the promises of God! God bless and much love.

# Daily Devotions

---

Good morning! Read Psalm 51:1–12 and James 4:7–10, then 1 John 1:6–10. We all have sinned! But our sinful past does not determine our future when we look to God and submit ourselves unto Him. It's the blood of Christ that cleanses us when we humble ourselves before God. It's the strength of the Holy Spirit in us that gives us strength to resist the temptation of sin when it crosses our path. It's by clinging to the Holy Spirit that helps us to shed our sin nature! It's the Holy Spirit that gives us hope for the future! God bless and much love.

# Daily Devotions

---

Good morning! Read James 4:1–10. God is willing to grant our desires but will hold back the blessing if we're not ready to receive it. To receive a 100 percent blessing, you must be 100 percent ready to receive it! It cannot be a desire to satisfy only you! It must be a desire that brings glory to God and being humble in the process. Not being selfish but understanding that those around you feel blessed for you. Especially the household of faith. By submitting yourself completely to God is the starting point to receive fully what God has for you. God bless and much love.

# Daily Devotions

———◇◇◇◇◇◇———

Good morning! Read Hebrews 5:11–14. One of the cutest things is watching a little child dress themselves. Their shoes are on the wrong feet. Their shirt is crooked, and their clothes don't match. But over time, they become skillful and learn how to dress themselves. Learning God's word is no different. Only with time spent do we become skillful in His Word. Our knowledge and understanding can only increase with time spent. Without taking that time, you are like that child trying to walk with shoes on the wrong feet. God bless and much love.

# Daily Devotions

———✦———

G ood morning! Read Psalm 103:10–18. The children of God are forgiven by God and their sins and transgressions are covered under the blood of Christ who took our past, present, and future sins and transgressions upon Himself on the cross. Not only are our sins and transgressions covered, but the stain of them are removed and cast away as far as the east is from the west! God understands our frailties and weaknesses! Be thankful for God's mercy and grace toward all who strive to be obedient to His Word! God bless and much love.

# Daily Devotions

———◇◆◇———

Good morning! Read Romans 10:17 and 2 Timothy 2:15. We are taught to read and write at an early age. As we grow, we become more skilled as our ability to read and write enables us to learn and understand many things. However, before we learned to read and write, someone had to speak the right words to teach us how. Growing your faith in God works much the same way! It's by hearing the Word of God that increases our faith! Faith that is increased even more by reading and understanding the Word of God! God bless and much love.

# Daily Devotions

---

Good morning! Read Luke 4:18–19 and John 8:31–36. Jesus Christ came to set the captives free! To free all who are in bondage and being held captive by the things of the world. Sadly and unfortunately, many do not realize they are in bondage and captivity! Living a life of limited resources apart from the unlimited resources of God! Living a lie and avoiding the truth of the Word of God! It's by knowing and living your life in the truth of God that opens the doors of freedom to the unlimited resources God has for you! God bless and much love.

# Daily Devotions

Good morning! Read 2 Corinthians 10:3–5 and James 1:13–16, then 1 John 2:15–17. The devil will send many temptations your way through the lust of the flesh, and the lust of the eyes, and the pride of life to turn your eyes and heart away from being obedient to God! It's important during these times of struggle that we look to God for strength to cast down these imaginations and bring them into captivity to the obedience of God in Christ! Although we live in the flesh, we must live a spiritual life in Christ! God bless and much love.

# Daily Devotions

———◇◆◇———

Good morning! Read 1 Timothy 4:8–11. There are many that have a regular workout program and eat a healthy diet in hopes of maintaining a healthy body and lifestyle. It's also important to live and maintain a healthy spiritual lifestyle. The exercising of our faith strengthens our faith in God. A daily healthy diet of His Word is nourishment to the body, soul, and spirit. This is profitable in all things so we can remain healthy and spiritually whole in Christ Jesus! Are you on God's workout plan today? God bless and much love.

# Daily Devotions

---

Good morning! Read Romans 1:17. Having faith in God goes far beyond what we hear and see. It's having the full belief and confidence in God no matter what we hear or see. God is able to lift us far above what seems logical in the natural realm of things. Having faith in the natural is one thing, but having faith in the supernatural ability of God goes beyond what's natural. It is this righteousness of God that is revealed from faith to faith! The just will live by faith! What level of faith do you live by? Yours or God's? God bless and much love.

# Daily Devotions

Good morning! Read Micah 6:8 and Hebrews 4:12. When we drive our car, the ride is bumpy and unpleasant when the tires are not balanced and out of alignment. It takes the right balance and alignment to have a smooth ride. The same is true in our walk with God. Our will must be in alignment with His will as we travel the road of life. It's not a partial alignment but a full alignment where His will is our will. Understanding the complete Word of God will give us the knowledge to know His perfect will for our life. God bless and much love.

# Daily Devotions

———◇◇◇◇◇———

Good morning! Read 2 Corinthians 5:7 and 2 Timothy 1:7, then 1 John 4:18–19. There is always apprehension to what is unknown. Having a fear of the unexpected can cause stress and anxiety to rise. This fear is conquered by our faith in God who knows what is unknown to us. What we can't see, God sees. Because He is light to light the way for all who put their trust and faith in Him. Having perfected His love in us to cast out all fear that we may live peacefully without worry. Walking by faith, not by sight! God bless and much love.

# Daily Devotions

———✦———

Good morning! Read Philippians 3:10 and 2 Timothy 2:15. It would be quite ignorant to form an opinion of someone without knowing them. You may know of them, but until you get to know them, an opinion really shouldn't be made. Yet many have an opinion of God and haven't taken the time to know Him. God is known by His Word! Not a chapter here or a verse there or what someone else says of God. It's by reading and studying the entire Word of God! Anything less is pure ignorance! Don't be ignorant, be informed! God bless and much love.

# Daily Devotions

---

Good morning! Read Micah 4:5 and Nahum 1:7, then Psalm 118:8. Many give God praise but are hesitant in giving Him their complete trust. Often deferring to the trusting in themselves or others. Having a form of worship but lacking the faith to firmly believe in God whom they worship. God knows who are His and those who have put their complete trust in Him. Those who put their trust in God know and understand God is their stronghold in whatever confronts them in life! God bless and much love.

# Daily Devotions

———✦◇◈◇✦———

Good morning! Read 2 Chronicles 15:7 and Galatians 6:9. Often many will start something but never finish whether it's a project, a workout program, a new goal, etc. They have the power to start but lack the staying power to continue. It's the staying power that's most important in completing what we've started! Having patience in our efforts is when we see the results and rewards for the work that we do. Relying on God for that added strength is often needed. It's His strength that gives us strength! God bless and much love.

# Daily Devotions

---

Good morning! Read Jeremiah 9:23–24 and John 14:6, then Romans 14:11–12. We live in a society where it's not what you know but who you know. It's not fair for those who have worked hard to achieve success to be passed over by someone who is not deserving because of who they know. In the eyes of God, it's do you know and believe in His Son. Knowing Reverend so-and-so or being friends with another Christian won't do it! But do you know Jesus Christ? You can't buy your way or talk your way into God's kingdom. Jesus Christ is the only way to God! Do you know Him? God bless and much love.

# Daily Devotions

───◇◆◇◆◇───

Good morning! Read 1 Corinthians 12:4–14. God has given us many gifts. The question is, are you using what God has given you? Each gift is to bless our life and for the building of the Body of Christ. Each of us are a building block and members one to another to lift and help each other as we, working together, with a common goal in lifting Jesus Christ as we are lifted by God in Christ. To ignore or not be aware of these gifts is like having the car of your dreams and not having the keys or having treasure that is lost. God bless and much love.

# Daily Devotions

---

Good morning! Read Matthew 7:7–11 and Revelation 3:20–22. Many are searching for answers about many things in life. However, it's by going to the right source to finding the right answers is most important. God is the source to the answers in life that is most relevant to each one of us. But you must seek God! When you ask, God will answer! If you seek, you shall find! When you knock, God will open the door of blessings! However, it first begins by you opening the door of your heart to allow God to enter your life! God bless and much love.

# Daily Devotions

———⬥⬥⬥———

Good morning! Read Matthew 14:26–31 and Mark 9:23–24, then John 14:12–16. One of the biggest problems for those who believe in Christ is their unbelief! They know and believe in God and the power in the name of Jesus Christ but fall short in total belief. However, God understands our short-comings of belief. God understands our belief is increased as we increase our knowledge and understanding of Him. As our belief increases, our doubts will decrease. Keep growing and keep learning to increase your belief! God bless and much love.

# Daily Devotions

---

Good morning! Read John 10:10 and Acts 2:46–47. The devil is a liar and the father of lies! His goal is to steal, kill, and destroy with his lies! The devil will also use the truth of your sinful past to make you feel unworthy of God's forgiveness. But as loud as the devil may speak, the Spirit of God speaks louder! However, you must have an ear to hear what the Spirit is saying to you! Understanding God adds to the church daily such as should be saved! Have you been saved by the grace of God? Do you hear His voice? God bless and much love.

# Daily Devotions

———◈◇◈◇◈———

Good morning! Read Nahum 1:7 and John 6:44–47, then 15:16. The opportunity to come to God is available to everyone. However, God already knows who trust Him and are open and willing to receive Him into their heart. These are who God has chosen and ordained to speak and teach His Word to others whom God has chosen that they who hear and believe will bear much fruit in their lives. God chose you long before you chose Him! But have you answered God's call? Well, have you? God bless and much love.

# Daily Devotions

---

Good morning! Read 2 Corinthians 10:3–6 and Philippians 2:5. Every day we all have battles to fight. But the first battle that must be fought is the battle within. The battle against depression, anxiety, self-control, pride, greed, wrong imaginations, or anything else that may be a shortcoming that may hinder the battles you face in life. To win the battles of life, you must first win the battle within! Putting on the mind of Christ is a must to win the battle within and fully equip you for the battles in life! God bless and much love.

# Daily Devotions

---

Good morning! Read Matthew 11:28–30 and Romans 1:16–17. God has an open-door policy. All who enter may bring all their burdens, worries, fears, doubts, concerns, and everything that keeps you from being whole. Inside you will find the righteousness of God that will shoulder all that has you weighed down. All who enter are cleansed and made new. Your worries and fears are replaced by faith. That faith is found in the gospel of Christ! It is the power of God unto salvation! Have you entered? God bless and much love.

# Daily Devotions

---

Good morning! Read 1 Corinthians 1:19–28 and 3:6. The greatest minds in the world cannot compare to the mind of God. We can count the seeds in the middle of an apple but only God knows how many apples are in the seeds when planted. A peach has one seed, but only God knows how many peaches that one seed will produce when planted. How much will God's Word produce in your life when planted in your heart? Nothing can grow unless its planted and watered. It's time to plant His Word to reap His harvest in due time. God bless and much love.

# Daily Devotions

---

Good morning! Read Malachi 3:6 and Romans 1:16–17, then Hebrews 13:8–9. We live in a world that is ever changing. But the one thing that has remained constant and has not changed is the Word of God! It is the same today as it was when God spoke His Word to the writers thousands of years ago. God's Word has not changed because God has not changed! The power of God is in His Word to all who believe! Its power has not diminished or changed, but it has the power to change all who believe! God bless and much love.

# Daily Devotions

G ood morning! Read Ephesians 1:17–19. Often many times in life we ponder the question of what our purpose is in life. Often we may feel lost like a ship lost at sea with no direction. However, when we look to God with a sincere heart, God will reveal your purpose in life in time. It's then that our purpose in life begins to have life! It's then that our eyes are opened, and the righteousness of God is revealed to us! It's then that we come alive in the purpose of our life! Knowing your purpose gives life to your life! God bless and much love.

# Daily Devotions

---

Good morning! Read Proverbs 4:20–27 and Luke 6:45–46. Just as the root nourishes a tree, the heart nourishes the soul and spirit. If the root dies, the tree dies, and without the heart, our soul and spirit are as good as dead. The devil is out to steal our hearts, so our souls and spirits are lifeless. But if we guard our heart and nourish it with the Word of God, we will continue to grow into living a godly life unto God. A good heart speaks good things. Our heart is the most important treasure we have! Guard it well! God bless and much love.

# Daily Devotions

Good morning! Read Matthew 11:28–30 and Luke 4:18–19. We all go through periods of stress, anxiety, and woes of different sorts. During these times, Jesus Christ is calling saying, "Come unto me!" Many look for a form of relief of these burdens while Jesus Christ is saying, "Come unto me!" Many are looking for the mending of broken hearts and deliverance from the problems of life. Searching for the freedom to live a life with contentment, peace, and joy. Jesus Christ has His hand stretched out saying, "Come unto me!" God bless and much love.

# Daily Devotions

Good morning! Read Genesis 15:5–6 and Matthew 17:1–5, then Hebrews 1:1–3. Before the Word of God was written, God spoke to His chosen, such as Abraham, through the stars and nature itself. The laws of God were written by Moses upon hearing from God Himself. Elijah and the many prophets prophesied and demonstrated His power by believing what was spoken to them by God. God revealed Himself to us in the body of His son Jesus Christ and has spoken to us through Him. Today is the day to listen and hear His voice. God bless and much love.

# Daily Devotions

---

G ood morning! Read Luke 7:41–43. Whenever we go on a long journey, we are always relieved when the long journey is over. The longer the journey, the more appreciative we are when we reach our destination. Those who haven't traveled as far cannot understand the length of the journey you've taken. Our life living in the Spirit of God is also a journey. It's also longer for some than for others. The longer the journey, the more you are appreciative of what God has done in your life. Always be thankful as you travel in this life! God bless and much love.

# Daily Devotions

———⟡⟡⟡———

Good morning! Read Deuteronomy 18:18 and Isaiah 7:14 and 53:1–5, then Daniel 9:25–26. The life of Jesus was foretold in the scriptures centuries before He came into the world. From His birth to His ministry until His death on the cross! The accuracy of the prophecies concerning Christ are right on point! Even the length of His ministry is detailed in scripture. Not only is the Word of God right about our Savior, but every prophecy concerning today's world events are unfolding right in front of our eyes! God bless and much love.

# Daily Devotions

———◈———

Good morning! Read Exodus 3:13–14 and Revelation 22:12–13. Every day has a beginning and an end. The sun rises and the sun sets. God is the Alpha and Omega. The beginning and the end of all things. It's important to know that God is not just the beginning and the end but everything in between. God told Moses His name is "I Am." Not "I Was" or "I Will Be" because God is all in all. From the beginning of days to the end of days, God is with us to help us, heal us, strengthen us, and to provide our every need. Praise Him daily! God bless and much love.

# Daily Devotions

***

Good morning! Read Nehemiah 8:10 and Romans 8:31–39, then Philippians 4:4. When we find joy in God, God finds joy in us. This joy comes from believing. When we have this joy, we see everything differently. Instead of sickness, we see health. We see the better and not the worse. Even in death, we are not separated but joined with God throughout eternity. Living a life above and beyond what is around us knowing God is for us to bring us through whatever is before us trying to keep us down. Seek and pursue His joy! God bless and much love.

# Daily Devotions

———⬦⬦⬦⬦———

Good morning! Read Matthew 17:5 and Hebrews 1:1–3. The words that Jesus spoke were more than just mere words. They were words that gave life to all who would apply His words to their life. From the words of the prophets before Christ to Christ and by way of the Holy Spirit today, God is still speaking to all who are willing to hear His Voice. It's when we listen and apply His words to our life that we receive guidance and instruction to live a renewed life in Christ! Do you hear Him speaking to you? God bless and much love.

# Daily Devotions

---

Good morning! Read Exodus 20:12 and John 15:11–16, then Romans 8:14–18. Abraham is called a friend of God. Until the time of Christ, the children of God were known as servants of God. Jesus Christ referred to those who believed in Him as friends. With the outpouring of the Holy Spirit, we have become sons and daughters of God. When we honor God as our Father, we fulfill the Fifth Commandment. This is the First Commandment with promise to be servants, friends, and children of God. Therein is the blessing! God bless and much love.

# Daily Devotions

———◇◇◇◇◇———

Good morning! Read Romans 8:1–10. There are two realms. There is the natural realm, and there is the spiritual realm. The natural realm can be seen, but the spiritual cannot be seen. We live in the natural realm, but the believers in God are lifted into the realm, which is spiritual by way of Jesus Christ. Not seeing but believing in the mighty power and mighty works of the Holy Spirit of God. We then see the results as God manifests Himself in our life. It's our choice in which realm we chose to live. What's your choice? God bless and much love.

# Daily Devotions

———⋄⋈⋈⋄———

Good morning! Read John 5:14 and Hebrews 10:26–31, then 2 Peter 2:20–22. When God has broken the chains of the bondage of sickness or delivered us from burdens that cause us to worry and given us the freedom to live in Him, the worse thing we can do is to take what God has done for granted. To go back to living the life from which God has cleansed us and made us new. To lay aside the understanding and knowledge we have gained of God. Only by staying true to God are we blessed by God! God bless and much love.

# Daily Devotions

---

Good morning! Read Isaiah 55:8–11 and 1 Corinthians 1:19–21. Throughout history, there have been many that have tried to prove or disprove the workings and wonders of God by scientific means. Not realizing that God does not live and exist totally within the realm and boundaries of science. The finite mind of man cannot fully understand the infinite mind of God. The greatest minds and wisdom of man is foolishness with God. What is the natural state of man cannot fully conceive the supernatural ways of God. God bless and much love.

# Daily Devotions

———◇◆◇◆◇◆◇———

Good morning! Read Ephesians 6:10–17 and Revelation 12:7–12. The phrase "misery loves company" is very fitting for Satan. Satan knows that his time is growing short and has a sense of urgency to steal, kill, destroy, and deceive as many people as possible. His mission is to take as many people down with him as he fights a battle with God that he knows he's lost. We must be prepared and not be ignorant of Satan's tactics but be suited with the armor of God to defend ourselves against his attacks. God bless and much love.

# Daily Devotions

---◇◇◇◇◇---

Good morning! Read Romans 6:3–10 and 10:9–13. For many, the changing of their ways is a struggle. To avoid the wrong things and the wrong people they are attached to can be a frustrating way to live life. Only God can replace the old you and create in you a new life in Christ Jesus! God can replace the wrong things and the wrong people with a new way of life having new things and new people that will help you in your spiritual walk in a new life. It begins by confessing and calling out to God that you may be saved! God bless and much love.

# Daily Devotions

———◇◈◇◈◇———

Good morning! Read Mark 11:24–26. Whenever we move, we get rid of what we don't need and keep the things that are of value. We also buy new things for the new place we are moving to. As this year comes to an end and we begin a new year, let's also get rid of what we don't need. Unforgiveness, selfishness, worries, doubts, and fears is what we don't need! Let's replace them with forgiveness, faith, compassion for others and a stronger love and a desire to know God! It's affordable! It's free! God bless and much love.

# Daily Devotions

———◇◇◇◇◇◇———

Good morning! Read Isaiah 35:3–4 and 40:3–8. Everything that has begun has an end. What's important is that what has begun has a strong finish. What God has begun in His children, He will surely give them a strong finish and more blessings in the latter end. But we must be strong and have continued strength in God and not falter in anyway or to anything that will cause us to doubt the promises in the Word of God. Although everything comes to an end, the Word of God will stand forever! God bless and much love.

# Daily Devotions

―――――◇◇◇◇◇◇◇◇―――――

Good morning! Read Ezekiel 18:20–28 and John 11:25–26, then 1 John 1:8–10. Everyone is born into sin. Unless we seek the forgiveness of God, our sins remain, and we will die in our sins. It's God's good pleasure that all live and seek His forgiveness and be cleansed from all unrighteousness. It's not our self-righteousness that saves us but the righteousness of God. We have a Savior in Jesus Christ that is the pathway to God. Without accepting Him and believing in Him, you cannot be saved. Through Christ is life! God bless and much love.

# Daily Devotions

———◇◆◇◆◇———

G ood morning! Read Exodus 20:12 and Ephesians 6:1–4, then Colossians 3:20–21. As children, we are commanded by God to obey our parents. As parents, we are instructed to not provoke our children to wrath but to raise and nurture them in such a way that they are not discouraged but are confident in their self-esteem with hope for a bright and prosperous future. It's the giving and showing of love between parents and children that is pleasing to God making Him the centerpiece of their lives! God bless and much love.

# Daily Devotions

———◇◇◇◇◇———

Good morning! Read Psalm 118:24. The sun rises to begin a new day and sets at the days end. Each day is precious and should never be taken for granted. We should make each day count for something positive that will enhance our life as we grow. The day we are born is like the sunrise, and the end of our life is like the sunset. Our life should not be taken for granted neither but should be filled with the positive things God has made available. To rejoice in this day of life God has made! Has your life counted? God bless and much love.

# Daily Devotions

———◇◆◇◆◇———

Good morning! Read John 6:32–40 and 44–51, then Romans 1:16. It's good to eat healthy to improve our physical health. However, the effects, as good as they may be, are only temporary. But spiritual health can lift our physical health to amazing heights when nourished with spiritual food. The gospel of Christ is the bread needed for this spiritual growth, which has unlimited potential. It's not a temporary fix but has everlasting results that cannot be measured. There isn't any better solution than the bread of life found only in Jesus Christ. God bless and much love.

# Daily Devotions

---

Good morning! Read Proverbs 4:20–23. The pieces of a puzzle must be completely put together to see and understand. All the pieces must fit perfectly! Often things that need to be assembled come with instructions. Without using the instructions, it becomes a guessing game on how to put the pieces together. Our life is like a puzzle with pieces that need to be assembled. The Word of God gives us the instructions to fit a broken and disassembled life back together again! However, you must first read the instructions! God bless and much love.

# Daily Devotions

---

Good morning! Read Matthew 12:33–37. Whatever seeds we plant in a garden is what will grow. Whether it's tomatoes or potatoes, peppers, or corn, whatever we plant is what will grow. This also applies to the seeds we plant in our heart! If they're seeds of hate, envy, resentment, or evil thoughts, that's what will grow in your heart! But if they're seeds of love, compassion, and good thoughts, that's what will grow in your heart! What comes from the heart exposes who we truly are! What's planted in your heart? God bless and much love.

# Daily Devotions

———◇◇◇◇◇———

Good morning! Read Mark 11:22–26. Our faith in God opens our eyes to hope. A hope and expectation that God hears and will answer our prayers in due time. Therefore, we can live our life with contentment knowing God is at work in our lives. However, we must also understand that the receiving of answered prayers comes with our unselfishness of forgiving others as God has forgiven us. Forgiveness is a two-way street! You must forgive to be forgiven! Forgiveness and faith put a smile on the face of God! God bless and much love.

# Daily Devotions

---

Good morning! Read Genesis 1:1 and Psalm 19:1, then Jeremiah 18:1–6 and Ephesians 2:10. We live in an ever-expanding universe. According to scientific experts, it's taken billions of years to evolve! Not understanding that length of time is a mere instant in the mind of God! Just as a sculptor admires their handiwork during their sculpting, God is admiring His creation and handiwork of a growing universe. You are God's workmanship and handiwork, and you are admired by God as you evolve and grow in Christ! God bless and much love.

# Daily Devotions

———✦———

Good morning! Read Genesis 2:7 and Psalm 51:7–13. God has breathed in us the breath of life that we might have life. A clean breath of life that our soul and spirit need to be heathy. But polluted air is not heathy for our body nor are polluted thoughts heathy for our mind, heart, and soul! It's so important to filter what we allow to enter our mind that's unhealthy to take root in our heart! However, God can cleanse us of a polluted mind and heart! God can also give us a new breath of life to live! God bless and much love.

# Daily Devotions

———◇◈◇◈◇———

Good morning! Read John 3:16–17 and 13:34–35, then 1 John 4:8–11. God is love! The height, width, and depth of the love God has for us is far beyond our understanding. God has loved us from the beginning, and His love will never fail! God loves us so much He sent His only begotten Son into the world to save the world from itself. And not only the world but to save you and I from ourselves! That we may express love toward one another to help save one another! It's all about love! God bless and much love.

# Daily Devotions

———◆◇◆◇◆———

Good morning! Read Psalm 90:12 and 118:24, then 2 Corinthians 4:14–18. Life is short! Our time of life is just a moment in time or a blip on the screen of life. It's important that we treasure the time we have in this life! Whatever afflictions we may go through or are going through cannot be compared to the weight of glory that awaits all who've put their lives in the hands of God! Although we may age outwardly, the inner Spirit of God renews our spirit daily. That we may strive and reach for the eternal things of God! God bless and much love.

# Daily Devotions

———⬦⬦⬦⬦⬦———

Good morning! Read 2 Corinthians 5:17 and Galatians 2:20. When the tires on our car are out of balance, the ride can be bumpy. When our car drifts to the right or left, it needs an alignment. There are many whose lives are out of balance and need an alignment! Just as repairs are needed for our car, our lives can be repaired through Christ! But for the repairs to be made, you must be in union with Christ! Your will must be in alignment with His will. The road in life can be bumpy, but the ride can be smooth with Christ! God bless and much love.

# Daily Devotions

———◈◈◈———

Good morning! Read John 15:16 and Philippians 1:6. Whenever we go grocery shopping, we handpick the best fruits and vegetables that are available. Those that are ripe enough to our perfection. We also handpick the best meats. The best trimmed and quality must be to our liking. God has also handpicked His children from among the billions that are in the world. Those who can be ripened in time to fulfill His will for them by Him. Are you ready to be chosen and handpicked by God? God bless and much love.

# Daily Devotions

———⬥⬥⬥⬥⬥———

Good morning! Read Isaiah 61:1–3 and Hebrews 11:6. God has taken the lives of imperfect people and turned their lives around. God has bound up the wounds of the broken-hearted, healed the sick and oppressed, and renewed hope to the hopeless. What God has done for others He can do for you! It's through our faith in God that operates in us that our lives are changed from what it was to what it is to what it can be! It's our faith in God that pleases God! But you must trust and believe! God bless and much love.

# Daily Devotions

———◈◈◈———

Good morning! Read Psalm 37:3–8 and Mark 11:24, then James 1:5–7. We all have desires and dreams we have in our heart. Dreams and goals we've had since we were children. But as we grow older, doubt creeps in, and we wonder if those dreams will ever be fulfilled. The first step is to remove the doubt! How? By turning to God and having delight in Him. Our trust in God can make the crooked path we're on in life straight. God is committed to us when we commit our life to Him. Not being envious of what others are doing but by being obedient to God. God bless and much love.

# Daily Devotions

---

Good morning! Read 1 Kings 8:27 and Psalm 104:1–5. God is small enough to live in our heart yet big enough that the heaven and heaven of heavens cannot contain Him. God's touch is on everything He created. From the thousands of different species of plants and animals to each snowflake and drop of rain. From the sun and moon to the millions of planets and stars in an ever-expanding universe, God's touch is there. God is all and is in all. Nature itself cries out and glorifies God for His handiwork. God bless and much love.

# Daily Devotions

---

Good morning! Read Proverbs 16:9 and Ecclesiastes 3:1–8. Each season throughout the year comes in its own timing. We cannot rush it nor delay it, and we prepare ourselves accordingly. We also go through seasons of growth through life! Our seasons of growth are known to God! To rush them or delay them delays the timing God has for the fulfillment and purpose He has for our life! We must look to God with diligence and patience and allow God to fulfill His purpose for us as we go through our seasons of growth! God bless and much love.

# Daily Devotions

---

Good morning! Read John 14:23–24. When we fall in love with someone, we do everything we can to learn more about them. We are at our best and do all we can to please them. It's a love affair we hope will endure for many years to come. Many declare that they love God but do very little to learn as much as they can about Him. Neither are they at their best or do the things to please Him. If you declare that you love God, strive to please Him as you would someone else! It's the greatest love affair we can have! God bless and much love.

# Daily Devotions

———◇◇◇———

Good morning! Read Isaiah 64:4. Disobedience to the Word of God and the voice of God has been from the beginning when God created Adam and Eve. Because of the continued disobedience, from generation to generation and the lack of patience, not willing to wait on God, many have not received what God has prepared for them. It's through obedience that our eyes are opened to God, and by having a listening ear do we hear what God has to say. Are your eyes open to the things of God? Do you hear? God bless and much love.

# Daily Devotions

---

Good morning! Read Luke 9:26 and Romans 1:16–17, then 2 Corinthians 3:2–3. As you walk in Christ, it is important that your walk be in the boldness of Christ. Not shamefully but in the power God as bestowed on us. We are to be living examples of the Word of God to others. Just as God revealed Himself in Christ, our life should reveal the presence of God in our words, actions, and conduct. Testifying of the power of God unto salvation to everyone that believes. God bless and much love.

# Daily Devotions

---

Good morning! Read Proverbs 16:1–3 and Ezekiel 18:26–32, then Romans 6:23. We have been taught right from wrong since childhood. As we grow and mature, it is our decision to choose to do right or wrong. God's will is for us to choose what is right. Sometimes the right choice can be a tough choice in today's world. But the wrong choice leads to bad consequences which must be faced at some point in life. God gives direction for what we ponder in our heart when we submit our lives to Him. God bless and much love.

# Daily Devotions

G ood morning! Read Ezekiel 3:17–21. The children of God are more than just children but also watchmen to warn the disobedient to turn from their wicked and sinful ways and to live a life of obedience to God. Whether they will listen or not, we have fulfilled our calling as being watchmen unto God! By doing so, we have delivered our own souls. Have you fulfilled your role of being a watchman to save the souls of others that they may receive the saving grace of God? God bless and much love.

# Daily Devotions

———◇◆◇———

Good morning! Read Matthew 11:28–30 and Philippians 4:11–13. As we go through life, we find ourselves in unfavorable situations and circumstances. However, we can still find contentment and comfort during these times when we look to God. It's knowing and understanding that whatever God's allows us to go through is for our growth. We always appreciate the mountaintop much better after we've gone through the valley! Just remember, we are not alone, but God is with us every step of the way! God bless and much love.

# Daily Devotions

Good morning! Read John 20:19–22 and Acts 2:1–4. Before the outpouring of the Holy Spirit, the disciples of Jesus were hidden in the upper room out of fear. But after the outpouring of the Holy Spirit, they were no longer afraid but came forth and spoke with boldness! Being born again of the Holy Spirit, we no longer have to fear, but we can live a life with boldness. We are not to suppress the spirit but express it in our lives. Having our doubts and fears conquered by faith in all we undertake! God bless and much love.

# Daily Devotions

Good morning! Read Psalm 62:1–2, then 91:1–6 and 9–12. When a ship has no anchor, it will drift according to the water's current. It must have an anchor to keep it in place. We also can drift if we don't remain anchored in the presence and promises of God. God only is our rock and our anchor to keep us from drifting to the currents that this world offers. To keep us securely fixed and safe when storms arise. Although the seas may be tossed, our anchor keeps us from moving because God is our anchor that we may not be moved. God bless and much love.

# Daily Devotions

---

Good morning! Read Jeremiah 17:5–8 and Matthew 4:4, then James 1:22–24. A glass house is transparent and easily broken. A brick house is a sturdy house. It helps keep heat in when it's cold and keeps it cool during times of heat. A brick house is built brick by brick. The more bricks you use, the bigger and stronger the house. The word of God are the bricks we use to build a strong sturdy life in Christ. Each word is a brick when heard or read; we make it a part of our life to build on to change our life. Let's start building! God bless and much love.

# Daily Devotions

***

Good morning! Read Psalm 17:8 and Zechariah 2:8, then Ephesians 2:10. When we keep God as the apple of our eye, we are kept as the apple of His eye! The benefits of being the apple of God's eye is immeasurable! We are showered and surrounded by His glory and righteousness. God's favor and blessings follow us everywhere we go and in everything we do. We are continuously nourished by the power of the Holy Spirit. God's workmanship at work creating in us according to His will in Christ Jesus! God bless and much love.

# Daily Devotions

---◈◈◈---

Good morning! Read Isaiah 54:17. For every problem we may face in life, God has a promise. If it's our health, God has promised to heal. If something has been lost or taken away, God has promised to restore. If your financial needs are overwhelming, God has promised to fulfill your need. It's by our complete trust and faith in God that His promises intervene in our life. When the things and problems of this world closes its eyes on you, keep your eyes open and look unto God! God is our problem solver! God bless and much love.

# Daily Devotions

————◇◈◇————

Good morning! Read Luke 12:8–10 and John 14:23–24. No one wants to be where they're not wanted. To not feel the love and respect we deserve even though we want their approval, love, and respect. It's far better to love and respect those who love and respect us. Only then can a friendship and relationship come to fruition. Our relationship with our Savior is more than a friendship. It is the most intimate relationship we can have when we accept Him as He is. After all, He's accepted us as we are! God bless and much love.

# Daily Devotions

———————◇◈◈◈◇———————

Good morning! Read 1 Samuel 17:42–47 and Isaiah 54:17, then John 8:28 and Ephesians 5:20. When we live a life that is pleasing and glorifies God, God in turn glorifies us. He is always with us! Our battles become His battles. Our victory is His victory. When we give God thanks, God is blessed and blesses us for our courage and thankfulness to Him. Whatever challenges we may face, we can be confident that we are not standing alone, but the power of God and God Himself is there to stand with us. God bless and much love.

# Daily Devotions

———◈———

Good morning! Read Ephesians 2:4–10 and 1 Timothy 2:3–5, then Hebrews 4:9–11. Experience is the best teacher. God wants all to experience what He teaches us in His Word. To walk and know the road to salvation is through Jesus Christ. To know that His grace is not by our works but is freely given to those that seek His grace. God wants us to find rest in Him so He can work in us. To be our strength in times we are weak. To bring us comfort and joy during times of sorrow. To bless us with His love. God bless and much love.

# Daily Devotions

---

Good morning! Read Job 28:12–28 and James 1:5–8. To make the wisest decisions takes wisdom. But wisdom without knowledge and understanding can be fruitless. There is nothing more valuable in life than having the wisdom to choose correctly and righteously. True wisdom cannot be bought! True wisdom comes from God who gives liberally to all who ask. But it must be asked in faith! Not doubting but having full assurance that God will give us the wisdom to discern in our decision making. God bless and much love.

# Daily Devotions

---✦---

Good morning! Read Psalm 119:9–16 and Romans 12:1–2. The Bible is an open love letter from God to the world. Have you read it? The Bible is a history book detailing His story from the beginning. Do you read it and know it? The Bible is a roadmap for the journey from the beginning to the end of the road of life. Are you lost and need direction? The Bible is a forecaster of today's and tomorrow's events. Are you prepared for what lies ahead? The Bible is a transformer that can change anyone that believes. Have you been transformed? God bless and much love.

# Daily Devotions

---

Good morning! Read Numbers 23:19 and Proverbs 4:20–23, then 3rd John 2. The Bible is the Word of God that fuels our faith. It empowers us to run the race of life and carries us to and through the finish line. Just as a car without gas cannot move, neither can the child of God without the Word of God. Just as you need a healthy lifestyle to live a healthy life, a daily healthy dose of God's Word is needed as well. It is the best remedy for a healthy heart, soul, and mind. Let the Word of God supply your strength and be your strength. God bless and much love.

# Daily Devotions

---

Good morning! Read Isaiah 40:28–31. As we get older, many go through different health issues. Often preventative measures are taken to maintain good health. Exercise and a healthy diet are always good. However, even those living a healthy lifestyle can have setbacks. Doctors and health physicians can give you recommendations, but only God can give you and restore in you the need that your health requires. Seek His face for guidance in your health needs. God is the builder and maker of us all! God bless and much love.

# Daily Devotions

―――――◇◆◇◆◇◆◇――――――

Good morning! Read Psalm 56:8–13. When we are in the favor of a God, His promises are always before us. His promise to keep us from falling and to deliver us from the will of those against us. When we put our complete trust in God, we have no fear to what others try to do to us. It's God's favor of grace that sustains us and strengthens us to withstand anything that may attempt to harm us. It's God's favor that enables us to be a light and an example as we shine among all who cross our path! Praise Him! God bless and much love.

# Daily Devotions

---

Good morning! Read Proverbs 30:11–14 and Isaiah 5:20–23, then 2 Timothy 3:1–5. There is change from one generation to the next. What was considered good and right is now deemed unfit for the generation of today. Although many profess a certain faith, their walk and actions deny what their faith is grounded in. Being led away from the root of love spoken of in every faith. God spoke of these changes hundreds of years ago. To get back to the root of love, this generation must turn back to God who is the founder and foundation of love. God bless and much love.

# Daily Devotions

---

Good morning! Read Romans 12:1–3 and Colossians 2:9–12. We upgrade things to be more productive—our car, computers, cell phones, etc. We upgrade our clothes and hairstyles to keep up with the times. Many need to upgrade their lives spiritually to *not* accept what is a natural upgrade but to upgrade to the ways and will of God which brings about supernatural change in our life. This spiritual upgrade is ever increasing to unlimited proportions which only God can offer and give. It's time to upgrade! God bless and much love.

# Daily Devotions

———◈❖◈———

Good morning! Read Colossians 3:1–4 and 16–17. If Christ lives in you, your affections are on heavenly things above and not on earth. It's the heavenly things that are eternal and add to what is spiritual within you. From within comes the Spirit of God working and shaping us according to His pleasure and will for us that we may be filled with godly wisdom as we grow in Christ. Teaching and encouraging one another in word and deed giving thanks and glorifying God with a joyful heart, soul, and mind! God bless and much love.

# Daily Devotions

---

Good morning! Read Proverbs 9:10 and Jeremiah 2:13 and 9:23–24, then Hosea 4:6. With education comes knowledge and understanding. With these, we are able to make rational decisions concerning our life. Whether it's our wealth or health, our education plays an important part. However, the wisdom to make the right decisions comes from accepting and knowing God. It's our desire to know and understand God that delights Him the most! When we understand God, we realize how much we are truly blessed! God bless and much love.

# Daily Devotions

---

Good morning! Read Revelation 19:7–9. There is always excitement for a wedding. All the preparations leading up to that big day are more than worth the efforts and work put into making it such a special day for the bride and groom. Having an invitation and acknowledging our attendance on that special day is thrilling to all. There is a wedding like no other coming one day. The wedding of Jesus Christ, the Lamb of God, and all believers, which is the church. Are you on the guest list? Do you have an invitation? Are you prepared to attend? God bless and much love.

# Daily Devotions

---

Good morning! Read Psalm 51:1–10 and Matthew 5:48, then Romans 3:23. We all have sinned and fallen short of perfection. It's impossible for us to be perfect, however, it is possible to strive for perfection. Giving all we have and doing the best we can to be the best possible person we can be. We were born on the wrong side of the tracks into sin, but God is able to cleanse us and give us a new start toward perfection. To perfect our trust and faith in God's Word is the goal we seek to find perfection through Jesus Christ. God bless and much love.

# Daily Devotions

---

Good morning! Read Genesis 3:6–10 and Micah 6:8, then 2 Corinthians 13:5–8. When Adam and Eve sinned, the spiritual connection with God died. God verbally called out saying, "Where are you?" God obviously knew but did they know? This is a question many need to ask themselves! Where are *you* in your spiritual life? Where are *you* in your knowledge of God? Where are *you* in your relationship with God? Where are *you* in your walk with God, or are *you* walking alone? Where are *you*? God bless and much love.

# Daily Devotions

---

Good morning! Read Proverbs 3:5–6. Often times we are advised to trust our instincts when we are uncertain of what direction to take or which way to go as we journey through life. When we put our life in the hands of God, we instinctively put our trust in Him. By acknowledging God to direct our way, the right way, and the right path is always before us. God will also bring the right people into your life at the right time and remove those who hinder your walk. But it's our instinctive trust in God that directs our way! God bless and much love.

# Daily Devotions

---

Good morning! Read Romans 8:28–31. Every child of God serves a purpose in God's plan. Often His children go through difficult times, but the end result are His blessings. Without the difficult times, we can't fully appreciate the blessings that follow. All was predestined in the mind of God from the beginning! And if predestined, then we were also justified. And if justified, then we also were glorified in Him. It doesn't matter how dark the hour may seem; our God is the light to lead the way! God bless and much love.

# Daily Devotions

---

Good morning! Read Isaiah 29:11–14 and James 4:8. God knows each and every one of us, and it is God's earnest desire that we read His Word that we may know Him. Too often many have excuses such as not having time or saying they don't understand the Bible or are not really sure what to believe, wondering if there is a God. Seeking the advice and opinion of others rather than seeking the written word of truth. Only by drawing close to God will God be drawn to you. No excuses! Try God! I dare you! God bless and much love.

# Daily Devotions

———◆◇◆◇◆———

Good morning! Read Exodus 20:12 and Malachi 1:6, then Hebrews 12:6–14. The Fifth Commandment, to "honor thy father and thy mother," is the first commandment with promise. The promise that thy days may be long when we honor our parents. In teaching us right from wrong some form of discipline was used. Although we may have experienced anger for a moment, our love was still intact. How much more should we love God who disciplines? God is our Father and giving Him honor is a promise that our days may be long. God bless and much love.

# Daily Devotions

---◇◆◇◆◇◆◇---

Good morning! Read Habakkuk 2:1–4 and Mark 11:24. When our will is in alignment with the will of God, our prayers are attuned to the things of God and obedience to God. Having a sure and confident faith in God, we can ask God in prayer with full expectation of having our prayers answered. Understanding that God's will for us is our will for ourselves! It's with patience that we wait knowing God's perfect timing for answered prayer will be perfect at a set and appointed time in our lives! Have faith! God bless and much love.

# Daily Devotions

---

Good morning! Read Isaiah 30:8–15. When a lesson is not learned, there is no growth! Without growth, there is no progress! There is very little or no progress in living your life without God. Yet many try and have tried to do so. Through this rebellion against God, they refuse to hear and obey the Word of God but satisfy themselves with what they want to hear. Their rebellion is not anything new but has happened many times in the past bringing ultimate destruction to many. Learn from the lessons of the past that you may grow! God bless and much love.

# Daily Devotions

---

Good morning! Read Genesis 3:1–5 and Psalm 12:6, then Hebrews 4:12. One of the ongoing ploys of the devil is to get the children of God to doubt the truth of God. Knowing doubt brings about fear, and both will weaken your faith! However, the truth of God confirms the Word of God! It is consistent from the Book of Genesis throughout the Book of Revelation! When you're focused on the Word of God in your life, it leaves very little room for the devil to distract you with his lies of deceit! God bless and much love.

# Daily Devotions

---

Good morning! Read Proverbs 17:6. We enter the circle of life the day we are born. As we grow, we learn new things and experience the many facets and adventures that life has to offer. There are high times and low times during our circle of life. From the fascination of watching our children grow up to their watching us age as we grow older. However, our children are our crown and the glory of our children are the parents. We are to find pleasure in life in our journey through the circle of life! God bless and much love.

# Daily Devotions

———◇❈◇◈◇❈◇———

Good morning! Read Romans 12:9–21. Retaliation does not bring peace, but it escalates the problem rather than solve it! One hand trying to outdo the other, so to speak! We are not to retaliate but to pray for our adversaries! Retaliation gives the devil a foothold on your situation and theirs. Deepening the wounds of all parties involved. However, putting all things into the hands of God gives God the control needed to subside the situations concerning all involved. Vengeance belongs to God! Give it all to Him! God bless and much love.

# Daily Devotions

---

Good morning! Read John 1:1–3 and 1 Timothy 3:16, then 2 Timothy 2:15. There are many who seek and profess their love for God yet spend little or no time in the Word of God. The Word of God was with God from the beginning and was God! God's Word was manifested (revealed) in the flesh in His Son Jesus Christ. Only by spending time in His Word do you come to know Him as He truly is. It's not what you've heard or what you may feel and think, but what you read, learn, and study for yourself! Do you know Him? God bless and much love.

# Daily Devotions

---

Good morning! Read Psalm 68:5. There are many children who grow up in broken homes. Being raised and taught by a single parent, whether it's the mother or the father, foster care, or adoption. There are also many who have lost their significant other, whether it's either the husband or wife and face living their life without the love of their life. However, we can always look to God who is a Father to the fatherless and will comfort the hearts of those who have lost their significant other! God bless and much love.

# Daily Devotions

————✦✦✦————

Good morning! Read Psalm 91:1–7. God has sanctified us and given us freedom through His Word. The devil wants to keep us captive in mind and soul. Jesus Christ is the key to the locked door of our mind. The door has been opened! All we have to do is walk through it. Many are like a caged bird that doesn't what to fly away when the cage door has been opened. Not realizing that he has been set free. Free to soar to greater heights than he's ever known. God wants us to soar to greater heights in this life and beyond. God bless and much love.

# Daily Devotions

---※◇◇◇◇◇◇◇※---

Good morning! Read 2 Chronicles 7:14 and Psalm 37:37, then Titus 2:1–8. As children, we had role models as an example on how to live. With aspirations to be like them as we grew older. Unfortunately for many this Pied Piper following led many down the wrong path. Only through humility can we turn our life around and move forward to a path that is a beneficial example for those watching us. But we must be an example to ourself first! Knowing we are doing God's will in our heart and mind because…we are being watched! God bless and much love.

# Daily Devotions

Good morning! Read Psalm 103:1–5. God is a miracle worker, and His miracles never cease. Each morning that you open your eyes is a miracle from God! Count your blessings! Every time you recover from an illness is a miracle from God! Count your blessings! The restoring of your spirit and soul and life itself is a miracle of God! Count your blessings! Everything that you have is a miracle from God! Count your blessings! Take time and reflect on what God has done for you, and count your blessings! God bless and much love.

# Daily Devotions

———◇◇◇◇◇———

Good morning! Read 2 Timothy 1:7 and 1 Peter 2:21–25. Whenever fear comes knocking on your door, answer the door with faith. When weakness comes knocking, answer with the power of God. When hate appears, conquer it with love. When confusion arises, use the soundness of mind God has given. When sickness occurs, remember, you've been healed by the blood of Christ! We are able because God gave His perfect Son to pay the perfect price that we may be perfected in Him! Praise Him! God bless and much love.

# Daily Devotions

———◇◆◇◆◇———

Good morning! Read Luke 8:5–15 and John 10:10. Whenever you hear the Word of God, the devil immediately comes in an attempt to remove and take away that which you've heard and replace it with other thoughts. Unless you're rooted in the Word of God, this is relatively easily done. The devil knows the power of the Word of God can change your life and give you insight and strength to defeat the tactics he uses to steal, kill, and destroy those who seek life in Jesus Christ. Stay planted and rooted in the Word of God! God bless and much love.

# Daily Devotions

———✦◈◈◈✦———

Good morning! Read Deuteronomy 5:7–10 and 13:1–8, then Isaiah 42:8. There are times when our spiritual loyalty to God is tested. Whether it's our family or friends, having the best intentions, will suggest that you may seek a psychic or palm reader or dabble in astrology, tarot cards, or simply to seek other god's rather than the one true God! It must be understood that it's the devil using others to lure you away from God. To steal God's glory and to steal your soul! Be wise in what you do and whom you serve! God bless and much love.

# Daily Devotions

———✦———

Good morning! Read Psalm 37:3–9. and 2 Corinthians 5:7. Our obedience to God shows our trust and faith in God, and it's by our trust and faith that we are obedient to God! Often we can't see nor understand with our natural senses, but it's the spiritual working of our faith that we have confidence in God working in our life. It's through our commitment to God and having unwavering trust that is our true delight in God! When we are truly delighted in God, God is truly delighted in us! God bless and much love.

# Daily Devotions

———◇◇◇———

G ood morning! Read Psalm 27:13–14. It takes a lot of patience to patiently have patience to wait on God. Many live very busy fast-paced lives and have very little patience in dealing with many things. Living a life whereas time is of the essence in many areas of their lives. However, it's having patience and waiting on God that slows time down and puts all things in our lives in an orderly fashion. God's timing is perfect timing! But you must patiently wait and look to God! God is patiently waiting on you! God bless and much love.

# Daily Devotions

———◇◈◇———

Good morning! Read Mark 13:32–37 and Revelation 3:20–22. Whenever we're expecting guests, we always clean the house. Having everything done before they come knocking at your door. We want to make a good impression for our guest. Do you take time to clean your heart, mind, and soul in anticipation of Christ Jesus knocking at the door of your heart? Are you ready for His arrival? No one knows the date or time of His arrival. Only God knows His timing! If you're not ready, then get ready! Listen for His voice in anticipation of His knock. God bless and much love.

# Daily Devotions

---

Good morning! Read Psalm 46:1–11 and Psalm 26:3–4. When we look at the world around us, we see turmoil, anxiety, and unrest. When we look to God, we find peace and rest. The world is continually trying to pull us down, but God's hand is there to lift us up. The world is constantly raining guilt and shame, but God's light is the sunshine of your life. We must pause and be still and know that He is God! Our trust must be in Him and Him alone! God is our refuge during these times of trouble! Trust Him! God bless and much love.

# Daily Devotions

---

Good morning! Read Judges 6:12–16 and 7:2–7. God can take the least of the least to overcome and defeat the greatest of the great. The story of Gideon found in the Book of Judges chapters 6–8 is a wonderful example of the demonstration and overwhelming power of God. What God did in Gideon's life, He is more than able to do it in ours. There is no need to hang your head down but lift your head up and believe with all your heart, soul, mind, and strength that it is God that causes us to triumph and not ourselves. Always with each victory giving God the glory. God bless and much love.

# Daily Devotions

---

Good morning! Read 1 Timothy 2:5–6. When we are locked hand to hand, a show of unity is seen by all. Being in unity is a force that displays agreement with one another. When we live our life locked hand to hand with Christ, it's a show of unity and agreement with Him. It also must be understood that it's the hand of Christ that is holding God the Father's hand that unifies us in agreement with Him. Christ Jesus has stretched out His hand to us that we may be unified with God! Have you taken His hand? God bless and much love.

# Daily Devotions

———◇◇◇◇◇———

Good morning! Read Jeremiah 2:13 and Hosea 4:6, then Philippians 2:1–5. The world is reeling to and fro as corruption breeds more corruption. Rejecting God and the knowledge of God and replacing His knowledge with self-knowledge. Removing God from schools, institutions, and our courthouses. Using the Bible as a symbolic gesture during its weighing of justice. Not seeking the wisdom of God for true justice. The true followers of Christ are the glue that is keeping this world from falling apart. Only God can restore what this world has lost! God bless and much love.

# Daily Devotions

---

G ood morning! Read Mark 12:29–31. The two greatest commandments Jesus gave were about love. To love God with all your heart, soul, mind, and strength and to love our neighbor as ourself. Love is the common thread to having peace with one another! Jesus is the true example of expressing love to all. His acts of forgiveness, healing, and praying for all is the example we need to follow. When our life is love based, we fulfill the two commandments given by our Lord! Is your life love based? God bless and much love.

# Daily Devotions

---

Good morning! Read 2 Chronicles 16:9 and Psalm 18:1–6, then Acts 13:22. God described David as being a man after God's own heart. In spite of all his troubles and turmoil in his life, David *always* looked to God and sought *only* God for deliverance. David understood that his strength lied in the strength of God. When our faith is strong in God, His faithfulness is strong toward us. Begin each day by seeking God for deliverance and strength to fight what challenges you each day. God bless and much love.

# Daily Devotions

---

Good morning! Read James 1:21–25. We treat and reward our children when they are obedient and do what they're told and what they've been taught. Some type of form of discipline is given them for their disobedience. God also disciplines His children for their disobedience and rewards them for their obedience! That we may not be just hearers of His Word but doers of His Word by applying His Word actively in our lives. It's by this action of doing that gives us understanding of God and His Word! God bless and much love.

# Daily Devotions

———◇◇◇◇◇◇———

Good morning! Read Revelation 3:20–22 and 21:23–27. Our life is but a moment and shadow in time. How we live in this moment is all we can see and know but it determines what comes next. Throughout time, God has called many into His light. Like any light, the closer you get, the brighter it gets and the larger the shadow around us. With God, this shadow is His presence around us. When God knocks at the door of your heart, open it, and let His light in. Remember, you only have a moment! God bless and much love.

# Daily Devotions

———◇◆◇◆◇———

Good morning! Read 1 Samuel 16:7 and 1 Kings 8:61, then 2 Chronicles 16:9 and Galatians 5:16. God is perfect and seeks those with a perfect heart to show His strength on their behalf. Although we are not perfect by nature (because of the sin of the flesh), we can keep our hearts perfect toward God. God knows we are weak in the flesh, but having a heart toward God will help you overcome the weakness of the flesh. It's a steady progression as we grow in the spirit to the perfecting of our heart toward God. God bless and much love.

# Daily Devotions

---

Good morning! Read Psalm 100:3 and Proverbs 16:1–3 and 9, then Jeremiah 18:3–6. Each day is a day of preparation for the next. Your current situation is not your final destination. Each day God is shaping and molding us to perfection to who He would have us to be. Take heart and find comfort in your trust and belief in the workings of God in your life. Always keeping in your heart and mind that it is He that hath made us, and not we ourselves. God has the blueprint and plan for your life in the palm of His hand. Stay with God, and the plan will be fulfilled. God bless and much love.

# Daily Devotions

---

Good morning! Read Joshua 24:2–3 and Matthew 5:13–16. When you are chosen by God, God will separate you and lead you away from people, places, and things that separate you from Him. That you may flourish in His spiritual light and be an example to those that seek Him but have yet to know Him. That whoever sees you doesn't just see you but that they see God in Christ in you. It's the Light of God in us that draws those to God. The understanding and knowledge of God follows those hungry for God! God bless and much love.

# Daily Devotions

———✦✦✦———

Good morning! Read Psalm 139:14–17 and 2 Corinthians 5:17–18. There are many who have struggled in life. Having their dreams crushed and having dwindling hopes about their future. Wishing they could start over again. To press Pause and Reset their life. To have a new beginning in life! This is possible when you submit your life to Christ! To pause and reset your life in Him! To leave the past in the past and to behold your newness of life in Christ Jesus! To be renewed and fearfully and wonderfully made by God! God bless and much love.

# Daily Devotions

———◇◇◇◇◇◇◇———

Good morning! Read Psalm 1:1–3 and John 15:1–9. As a vine tree grows, its branches bring forth leaves and fruit. At the end of its season of life, the leaves begin to fade and fall and the vine begins to yield less fruit. This season of life is similar to our lives. We grow and bear fruit in our lives and toward the end of our season of life, we start losing friends and loved ones like leaves falling from a tree. However, those attached to the true vine of Christ shall be blessed and continuously bearing fruit! God bless and much love.

# Daily Devotions

———◇◆◇◆◇———

Good morning! Read Psalm 37:3–9. Everyone has dreamed and had thoughts of the kind of person they'd like to be and the kind of life they'd like to live. However, many lack the resources or skills to accomplish the life they'd like to live. But when we commit our life to God and put our trust in Him, our dreams and thoughts will become small in comparison to what God can do in your life. It's having delight and patience in God that greater things can happen far more than we could ever imagine! God bless and much love.

# Daily Devotions

---

Good morning! Read Isaiah 1:11–20. God hears all prayers and knows the intents of our heart and mind. Although God knows all things, it must be understood that He does not acknowledge the prayers of the disobedient because He knows the intents of their deceitful heart and mind. It's by sincere repentance that moves God to acknowledge and wash and make you clean from your disobedient ways that your prayers will be in good standing with God. However, your refusal will distant your prayers from God! God bless and much love.

# Daily Devotions

———◇◆◆◇———

Good morning! Read Matthew 6:24 and Luke 16:10–13, then Philippians 3:13. God has moved us from one side of the fence to the other. Yet many God has moved keep looking back to the other side of which they have been delivered. Not seeing the beauty of God's deliverance. You cannot move forward if you keep looking behind! Your faith cannot grow unless you seek the face of the One from which faith comes! God increases faith to the faithful. The true riches of God come to those who look and put their trust in Him! God bless and much love.

# Daily Devotions

---

Good morning! Read Psalm 37:37 and Proverbs 13:20. Many are judged by the company they keep! Often the road the company we keep travels, we will also follow. If we follow those who are wise, we become wiser. If we follow those who are foolish, we become foolish as well. Our associations can cause us to grow, or they can stunt our growth! However, the wisdom of God will guide you into associations that will enable you to grow when you seek His direction. It's then we find that perfect peace we desire to have! God bless and much love.

# Daily Devotions

Good morning! Read Psalm 16:5–9. Often we inherit the thoughts and beliefs of our parents, friends, or what we've learned over the course of a lifetime. It becomes so imbedded in our heart and mind whereas it also has become our thoughts and beliefs. When we look to God, we begin to inherit His thoughts and His ways become imbedded in our heart and mind. It's God's ways that begin to instruct us in our way of life. It's then that we rejoice and rest in hope! It's then we are assured we are blessed by Him! God bless and much love.

# Daily Devotions

G ood morning! Read 1 Samuel 30:6 and 1
Corinthians 15:57, then Galatians 6:9.
There comes a time in life when we are hit by
discouragement, fear, and doubt. Seeing the
door God has opened for us, but we are hesitant to go through. Much like the Israelites
hesitation at crossing the Red Sea. During
these times, we can find strength and encouragement in God who gives us strength and
direction. Understanding that we are victorious in Christ and hold the Word of God as
our staff to part our Red Sea of life that we
may cross over. God bless and much love.

# Daily Devotions

---

Good morning! Read Romans 10:17 and James 1:22–25. Our faith in God begins with hearing the Word of God. Our faith grows when we are actively applying the Word of God in our lives. It's a vital necessity that we are not just hearers of God's Word but also doers of God's Word that builds and increases our faith in our spiritual life! There can be no spiritual growth without spiritual application of God's Word in your life! When we apply God's Word in our life, the blessings of God will follow! God bless and much love.

# Daily Devotions

Good morning! Read 2 Kings 5:10–14 and 2 Corinthians 12:7–10. God is the Great Physician that can heal all things! However, God also wants us to be actively involved quite often in our healing process and not just sit back and do nothing. We must also do what we can to take care of ourselves. God will give us direction in what to do and who to see as we go through our healing process. God will give us the strength to endure! God is there in our time of weakness! But we must be actively involved! God bless and much love.

# Daily Devotions

———◆◇◆◇◆———

Good morning! Read John 6:35 and 47–51. The gospels have recorded many of the miracles performed by Jesus Christ. From turning water into wine to feeding thousands with a few loaves of bread and a few fish to healing the sick and much more! The miracles performed so long ago by Jesus Christ are being performed today in the lives of many who believe and have faith in His Name! Jesus Christ is the bread of life and restores life to all who put their trust in Him! When you believe, miracles happen! God bless and much love.

# Daily Devotions

---

G ood morning! Read Matthew 7:1–2 and Luke 6:37–38. There are many who pass judgment on others according to their view of life or their own personal feelings. Not fully understanding that judgment belongs to God. Nor understanding that with what judgment you judge, you shall be judged! Just as with karma, what goes around, comes around! It's God's will that we love one another in spite of our differing views and feelings and not judge others because of the difference! We're to love, not judge! God bless and much love.

# Daily Devotions

———◇◆◇◆◇———

Good morning! Read James 1:17–25. God has given us every good and perfect gift from above. His greatest gift is His Word that leads to life everlasting to all who receive and obey His Word. Receiving and hearing God's Word is one thing, but putting it into action in your life is another. Deceiving oneself by living according to their own personal will. Not accepting the complete Word of God but only what fits into their life. Not understanding that by denying the compete Word of God you are denying God. A glass half full is also half empty! Be full! God bless and much love.

# Daily Devotions

———◇◈◇———

Good morning! Read Romans 1:16. Every day is a new day and a day to show appreciation and give praise to God. It's a day where we have another opportunity to live our life with boldness in Christ. To share the good news of His gospel to those near and far. That the lives of others may be touched by His words through us. That salvation may come to all who believe the gospel of Christ! That the power of God may rest on them and be the encouraging words needed to bring change in their life! God bless and much love.

# Daily Devotions

———◇◇◇◇◇———

Good morning! Read John 15:1–10 and Romans 8:28. Everyone goes through some type of failure. However, failure isn't failure if you've learned from the experience. Many times God will allow things to happen in our life not for us to be defeated but through the process we may grow. When a tree is pruned, it is cut back so in process of time, it will bear more fruit. We are like a tree, and God does the pruning. What God is doing is a blessing in progress. Trust and be strong in faith! God bless and much love.

# Daily Devotions

---

Good morning! Read 2 Corinthians 6:14–18. When friendships develop, there is a bond that brings us closer together. However, we must be careful who we bond with in friendships. Is their belief in agreement with yours? Are they willing to do for you what you're willing to do for them? Are they walking in the Light of God as you are? Oil and water cannot be mixed, and neither can the believer in God sustain a meaningful lasting bond with an unbeliever! Be wise in whom you bond with! God bless and much love.

# Daily Devotions

---

Good morning! Read Genesis 9:12–16. A rainbow contains many colors and shades of colors that make up its beauty, yet the rainbow is one. Always appearing during and at the end of a storm. It is a reminder to God of His covenant He has with us. A sign of the mercy and grace He has promised to mankind. That we are to be one with Him and as one with one another. Although we are people of many colors, we should be like that rainbow. Full of beauty and as one in agreement with God and each other! God bless and much love.

# Daily Devotions

———◈———

Good morning! Read Proverbs 30:5–6 and Hebrews 4:12, then Revelation 22:18–19. There are some who pick and choose what to believe and what not to believe in God's Word. Essentially altering God's Word to fit their life and belief. They will add to and take away the parts that make them feel good in their own eyes. God's Word is not a suit that can be tailor made to fit your life! But you must have your life tailor made to fit God's Word! Does your life need to be altered to fit God's Word? God bless and much love.

# Daily Devotions

---

Good morning! Read John 14:6. We all live in different places and travel to work or school by taking the fastest shortest route to get there. Getting to the main road that leads to our destination. Although there may be several roads, there is only one road that we must eventually get on to get us there. To get on the main road that leads to God, we must travel the road of Jesus Christ. Only through Jesus Christ can we be led to God. Make no mistake! Christ is the way, the truth, and the life! There is no other way to the Father but by Him! God bless and much love.

# Daily Devotions

———◆◇◆◇◆———

G ood morning! Read Deuteronomy 8:10–20. During times of crisis and trouble, many seek God for answers and direction and deliverance. Unfortunately, many also forget about God and put Him on the back burner, so to speak. Having their heart lifted up and taking the credit when the credit should be given to God. Not realizing that whom God has exalted He is also able to bring down. It is His power that makes success possible! It's so important to stay humble and give God thanks in all things! God bless and much love.

# Daily Devotions

—◇◇◇◇◇◇—

Good morning! Read Joshua 10:12–14 and 2 Kings 20:1–11, then Psalm 90:1–14. Who controls time and the length of the days of our life? Whose existence is timeless? Who has all things in the Palm of His hands? No one but God and God alone! To think otherwise is not wise at all. The dog wags the tail. The tail doesn't wag the dog. God's mercies and grace are everlasting, and His gifts are endless and cannot be numbered. Call upon God for length of days, health, and His endless gifts. God bless and much love.

# Daily Devotions

———◇✕◇✕◇✕◇———

G ood morning! Read Proverbs 16:18 and 18:12. It's a good thing to have balance in our life. However, for many there is a great unbalance concerning their needs and wants. Their wants greatly exceed their needs, and their needs have taken a backseat to their wants. Pride is the centerpiece in this unbalance and is the cause of destruction for many! Balance is wanting what you need and needing what you want in your humbleness. Being humble begins with submitting to God! Are your wants and needs in balance? God bless and much love.

# Daily Devotions

---

Good morning! Read Romans 8:28–31 and Ephesians 1:4–12. The promises God has made God has kept. Not one word has fallen without its purpose being fulfilled. God has us in one hand and our purpose and destiny in the other. Bringing one hand to the other over time that we may be all in all. Fulfilling His plan which was in His mind before the foundation of the world. To give all His children an expected end. Rewarding our hopes and dreams because of obedience and faith in Him. Only by staying in His hand can God fulfill His plan for you! God bless and much love.

# Daily Devotions

---

Good morning! Read Psalm 118:24. Our attitude and outlook set the course of the beginning of each day. A positive thought in beginning the day is the right attitude to have. Not living in yesterday but leaving yesterday in yesterday and living and enjoying life today in today! Each day is another day God has made and blessed us with that we may rejoice and be glad in it! However, the greatest and wisest attitude and outlook is taking God into each day with you! Making God a part of your day will make your day! God bless and much love.

# Daily Devotions

———◇◈◇◈◇———

Good morning! Read 2 Chronicles 30:9 and Isaiah 55:6–7 and 59:1. Like a ship drifts from shore when it's not anchored, believers in Christ can drift from God, being lured away by the things of this world. It's necessary to take the time to regroup and reestablish our priorities. God is patient and will never turn His back and say no. His mercy and grace is sufficient enough to cleanse and restore us to where we need to be. God can remove the shame felt and return us to the joy of His salvation. God bless and much love.

# Daily Devotions

———◇❈◇———

Good morning! Read Ephesians 4:29–32 and 1 John 4:1. With the internet and social media, we are able to reach virtually every corner of the world, providing information and ideas in a range of topics with worldwide access. However, many are using this service to slander and prey on others for their own benefit! Being led by a spirit that *is not* of God but by the wicked spirit of the devil! However, those of God will use this service to edify and build and lift each other up! Let's use the internet to help others and not hurt! God bless and much love.

# Daily Devotions

———◇◈◇———

Good morning! Read Ephesians 4:29–32 and 1 John 4:1. With the internet and social media we are able to reach virtually every corner of the world. Providing information and ideas in a range of topics with worldwide access. However, many are using this service to slander and prey on others for their own benefit! Being led by a spirit that *is not* of God but by the wicked spirit of the devil! However, those of God will use this service to edify and build and lift each other up! Let's use the internet to help others and not hurt! God bless and much love.

# Daily Devotions

---

Good morning! Read Hebrews 11:1–6. It takes very little faith to believe in what we can see. It takes very faith to believe in a sure thing or when the odds are in your favor. However, true faith is having hope and belief in the evidence of things not seen! To having trust and belief in an unseen God is the true essence of faith! Having faith in God we believe and know that in spite of the odds against us, with God, the odds are now in our favor. It's through our faith that we diligently seek God and find rest and confidence in Him! God bless and much love.

# Daily Devotions

---

Good morning! Read 1 Thessalonians 4:13–18. While we are young, we have the excitement of our youth. The birth of children, weddings, and memories we share with family and friends. Memories we cherish all our days. As we grow older, we mourn the passing of family members and friends but hold on to the memories knowing one day we will see them again in God's kingdom. Cherish each family member and friend because one day they will be a memory for you or you will be a memory for them. God bless and much love.

# Daily Devotions

---

Good morning! Read Isaiah 26:3–4 and Philippians 4:6–7, then 1 Peter 5:7. Everyone hopes for world peace as we live day to day in a world filled with conflict and turmoil. Although world peace has eluded the world, there can be peace in the life you live. This peace is not just any peace, but it's having perfect peace when your mind is stayed on God! It's God's caring love that sustains us during our times of trouble. It's God's caring love that keeps our hearts and minds through Christ Jesus! God bless and much love.

# Daily Devotions

———◈✕✕✕✕✕✕◈———

Good morning! Read Matthew 25:31–46. Jesus was and is passionate and shows compassion for each one of us, and His desire is that we do the same to and for one another. As He has been, so are we to be to others. Showing love and concern and helping the less fortunate in their time of need. If someone is hungry, we feed them. If they are sick, we comfort them. By forgiving, we are forgiven. We will be judged by the intents of the heart. Therefore, prepare your heart to have the heart of Christ! God bless and much love.

# Daily Devotions

———◇◈◇———

Good morning! Read Psalm 103:13–18. God knows that our life is short on this earth. God knows and understands how frail we are and that we need His mercy and grace to sustain us and help us during our short time here. God gives strength to the weak and comfort to those who are afflicted and seek His righteousness and desire to know Him. The blessings of God's peace will shadow all who walk in His ways of obedience to Him. It's our understanding of God that opens our eyes to His glory! God bless and much love.

# Daily Devotions

---

Good morning! Read Genesis 4:8–10 and Romans 8:15–18. When God questioned Cain concerning Abel, his response was, "Am I my brother's keeper?" Well the truth is we are our brother's keeper. Being children of God and joint heirs with Christ, we are kept in God by way of Jesus Christ. Christ is our Keeper and Shepherds His sheep. We are to shepherd and love one another in the same manner. Not like Cain who slew his brother because of envy and jealousy. God bless and much love.

# Daily Devotions

———◆◆◆◆◆———

Good morning! Read Isaiah 14:12–20 and Ezekiel 28:13–19. God gets blamed for the world's misery. For death and destruction which God does not cause. Hurricanes and earthquakes are referred to as an act of God. Not understanding who's really behind it. Blinded by the master of disguise Satan himself. When any crime is committed an investigation is needed to find the truth. Satan is exposed in the word of God and will do everything to hinder your investigation. *Investigate!* God bless and much love.

# Daily Devotions

Good morning! Read Ecclesiastes 4:9–12 and Matthew 11:28–30. We turn our palms up to hold things. However, at times some things are too heavy, and we need assistance to carry the load. When life's worries become too heavy to carry its load, we can turn our hands over, palms down, and release the weight of life into God's hands! It's then we can return our empty palms face up to now receive the help and blessings of God! Replacing the weight of life with palms up to worship, thank and praise God! God bless and much love.

# Daily Devotions

———◇◈◇———

Good morning! Read Nehemiah 8:10 and Micah 6:8, then Hebrews 11:6. One step leads to the next! And with each step, we move farther from where we were and closer to where we desire to be. The most important steps we can take are taking steps of faith in God! Having these steps of faith is what's pleasing to God as God is also walking with us on our journey in life. It's then that you realize that the joy of the Lord is your strength! However, the steps of faith must be taken! God bless and much love.

# Daily Devotions

Good morning! Read Luke 9:23–24 and Philippians 4:4–7. Following Jesus is something we must do daily. Laying aside our life and finding new life in Him. Living a new life with faith and confidence knowing that what is meant for us we will receive. Believing our prayers and supplications and requests are heard by God when our life is in alignment with His will. Trusting Him we find peace and rest in Him as we patiently wait to receive the rewards God has for us. But we must follow Him! God bless and much love.

# Daily Devotions

---

Good morning! Read John 16:33 and Titus 1:15–16, then Jude verses 17–25. There isn't any doubt that we live in a world filled with chaos. Chasing after things that are not of God. But the followers of Jesus Christ can rest assured because as Christ overcame the world so shall we if we continue to abide in Him. Our faith is our strength during these times of tribulation. Professing our faith through our works having our minds pure and building ourselves up on our most holy faith knowing our God will keep us from falling. God bless and much love.

# Daily Devotions

---

Good morning! Read Proverbs 16:9 and John 16:13. A farmer never puts the cart before the horse. After all, it's the horse that pulls the cart, and the farmer directs the horse in the right direction to pull the cart. We are like that cart, and the Holy Spirit is like that horse, and God is like that farmer to direct our way. It's God who leads us beside sill waters and restores our soul! Let's *not* get ahead of God but allow God to direct our way through His Holy Spirit as we journey through life! God knows the direction we should take! God bless and much love.

# Daily Devotions

---

Good morning! Read Isaiah 41:10 and 43:1–2 and 2 Corinthians 5:7, then Hebrews 11:1–3 and 6. God has promised to be faithful to the faithful. To be faithful means to be full of faith! Having unwavering faith that God is with us to guide and deliver us in the most difficult times. Giving us hope that even though we don't see the outcome we know God does and has already made a way. It's our faith that sustains us! It's our faith that moves God, and God moves us through the fire and storms of life so we will not be burned or overcome. We are never alone. God is always with us. God bless and much love.

# Daily Devotions

---

Good morning! Read 2 Corinthians 6:14–18 and Romans 6:23. As parents, we try to keep our children from bad influences and running with the wrong crowd. God wants the same for us. Bad influences and the wrong crowd can lead you down the wrong path. As enticing as something may seem, we must be wise enough and strong enough to turn away. God can give us the wisdom and strength to do so. No matter how strong you may think you are, sin is stronger. God bless and much love.

# Daily Devotions

---

Good morning! Read Matthew 18:21–22 and Mark 11:25–26, then 1 John 1:8–10. It's difficult to forgive someone who has hurt you. However, forgiving frees you from the weight of unforgiveness! Not forgiving is like slicing your own wrist and waiting for the other person to bleed out! No one is perfect and sin free, yet Christ died for our sins! We have been forgiven, and we are to be forgiving! If you are forgiving to others, God will forgive you! Otherwise, the weight of unforgiveness will weigh you down! God bless and much love.

# Daily Devotions

---

Good morning! Read Ezekiel 36:23–27 and 1 Peter 1:23–25. The advances of science are growing at an alarming rate. From blood types to DNA, no two are the same. Similar but different. We get our DNA from our parents. When we are born again, we receive the DNA of God, which is His Holy Spirit. This DNA is also similar but different according to the spiritual gifts God gives us. The DNA of God carries no disease nor aging process but renews our spirit unto eternal life in Christ Jesus. God bless and much love.

# Daily Devotions

---

Good morning! Read Matthew 13:3–9 and 18–23. There are many who hear the Word of God and joyfully receive the Word of God. Yet there are also many who have doubts and question not only the Word of God but the very existence of God Himself. It's only through the belief in God and seeking understanding and the knowledge of God through His Word that the blessings of God are manifested in your life. Only then is the fruit of the Spirit multiplied! If you plant the seed of His Word in your heart, it will grow! God bless and much love.

# Daily Devotions

———◇◇◇◇◇◇◇———

Good morning! Read Matthew 24:3–14. The Bible is very detailed about the end times. The words of Jesus Christ, although spoken two thousand years ago, are so prophetic as though they were spoken today. Wars and rumors of wars, the persecution of Christians, and those of other beliefs. The ever presence of cults and hate groups. The lack of respect for parents and the coldness of heart toward others. Stronger and more frequent earthquakes and storms. Just think… This is only the beginning of sorrows. Stay in prayer! God bless and much love.

# Daily Devotions

———◇◈◇———

Good morning! Read 1 Corinthians 12:4–27. Every house that is built has an architect to design the house. Someone skilled to lay the foundation and build the walls. Another to do the electrical and another to lay the pipes for the plumbing and so on. Each one must work together in building the house to make it complete. They all are important one to another! We have been given different spiritual gifts for the building of the Body of Christ whose architect and designer is God! Each one of us must do our part! God bless and much love.

# Daily Devotions

———◇◇◇◇◇———

Good morning! Read Matthew 10:19–20 and 1 Peter 3:15. When your heart and mind are in alignment with God, God's thoughts become your thoughts, and God's words become the words you speak. When you are in alignment with God, the message you speak to others is in effect the message of God! It's important that you yield to the thoughts of God and the words of God for the message to have its full effect on all who hear. Having a ready answer in defense of your faith and the gospel of Christ! God bless and much love.

# Daily Devotions

———◇◇◇◇◇———

Good morning! Read Leviticus 26:3–9 and James 4:1–3. We reward our children for doing good and even reward our pets when they are obedient. The rewards we can expect from God are much more satisfying than anything we could ask or think. Just as we are proud of our children's obedience to our word, God is proud of His children's obedience to His word. Granting our desire in time when our desire is not to fulfill our personal lust but the desire that brings glory to God. Having glorified God, we obtain His glory in our life. God bless and much love.

# Daily Devotions

———✦———

G ood morning! Read 1 Chronicles 17:26–27 and John 10:10. God has adorned us with His blessings and made His precious promises available to us. But it takes complete trust and faith to receive what God has promised. God eagerly wants to bless us with an abundant life according to His will. Abundant living is not materialistic living but spiritual living. Reaching a level of spiritual maturity that cannot be matched by anything that we know. Exercising the powers that be of God. God bless and much love.

# Daily Devotions

---

Good morning! Read Matthew 6:9–15 and Mark 14:36. We face many challenges daily. The greatest challenge we face is doing our will or the will of God. God's will is that we love one another, to forgive one another, to help one another, and to live a life that is pleasing to Him. Jesus did all these and more and was subject to the Father as an example for us and to us. Being obedient to God demonstrates our love for God when do the will of God! Are you ready to meet this challenge today? God bless and much love.

# Daily Devotions

G ood morning! Read Proverbs 3:5–7 and Jeremiah 29:11–13, then Galatians 6:9. Sometimes we go through trials we don't understand. When our trust and faith in God are tested! Where there may be a physical or financial setback or any other type of setback when we are so desperately trying to move forward in life. When we endure the trial or test, our trust and faith is rewarded by God, and our setback becomes a setup for something better. Our hope is not in what we see but our hope is in God! God bless and much love.

# Daily Devotions

Good morning! Read 1 Corinthians 15:50–58. There is always constant change. From one season to the next, the weather constantly changes, and from one day to the next, we change in some way. We become stronger in some ways as we mature as we grow, but the greatest maturity is how we grow in Christ. This maturity and change leads to eternal life. It is through Christ that we will one day put off the corruptible for the incorruptible. It is Christ who conquered death that we may live. It is important that we be steadfast in our faith and unshakable in our belief. God bless and much love.

# Daily Devotions

———◇◇◇◇◇———

Good morning! Read Ephesians 1:3–5 and Revelation 13:8. Whenever a plan is made, there is a beginning and a desired result for the end. Before the creation and foundation of the world, God had a plan in mind with a beginning and a desired result. Even a plan of salvation was in the plan of God for all who believe in Him. A plan within a plan, so to speak! Each one of us are in God's plan with a purpose! There is a purpose for your purpose in God's plan! Nothing God plans and allows is without purpose! It's part of His plan! God bless and much love.

# Daily Devotions

---

Good morning! Read Proverbs 3:5–6. Whenever God removes you from somewhere or from certain friends, He will lead you to another place and other friends that will help you grow to fulfill the plan He has for you. But you must trust Him with all your heart and lean not unto your own understanding. You must acknowledge God in all your ways through your faith in Him and allow Him to direct your path in this journey of life. When God removes you from somewhere, He is drawing you closer to Him! Trust Him! God bless and much love.

# Daily Devotions

———◇◇◇◇◇◇◇◇———

Good morning! Read Proverbs 24:16 and Luke 15:10. We all are joyful when a baby takes their first steps. We say things like "Come on, come to me!" When they fall, we lift them up and encourage them to keep trying. God and the angels in heaven are joyful when anyone seeks God and takes steps of faith to Him. When we fall, God will lift us up and give us signs of encouragement. As the baby's steps get better and stronger, we get better and stronger in our steps of faith as we grow in the Spirit! God bless and much love.

# Daily Devotions

---

Good morning! Read Exodus 23:20–22 and Matthew 16:24–25. As children, we played a game called follow the leader. The one leading would lead us through various turns and detours, and we followed them. Jesus Christ has asked us to follow Him! To deny ourselves and to take up His cross, and follow Him! When we do, Christ will lead us through the various turns and detours that life throws our way. However, we must deny ourselves to find new life in Him! It's in our new life that we follow Him! God bless and much love.

# Daily Devotions

———◇◇◇◇———

Good morning! Read Psalm 37:23–24 and Proverbs 24:16. Many have the intention of living right and doing right. However, at times, we fall short and misstep the steps we are trying to make. Although we may fall short and make mistakes, our efforts are delightful in the eyes of God. God will lift us up when we fall and give us the strength and motivation to take another step. But before you take the next step, you have to take the first step, and that first step must be to God. God in turn will direct your steps in the way you should go. God bless and much love.

# Random Thoughts

- If you're hurting, don't bite and hurt the hand that's trying to help you! Just a random thought!

- The love we express outwardly is an expression of the love we feel inwardly! Just a random thought!

- Lies can be hurtful! Truth can also be hurtful when it exposes the lies! Just a random thought!

- A leader who is blind to the truth will blindly lead their followers away from the truth! Just a random thought!

# Random Thoughts

- We've all cried tears of sorrow! However, God can turn your tears of sorrow into tears of joy! Just a random thought!

- The devil will weaken your faith through fear! God will weaken your fear through faith! Just a random thought!

- God may not give you what you want, but He will give you what you need…often before you know you need it! Just a random thought!

- Small steps of faith in God lead to bigger steps of faith in God! But you have to take the steps of faith! Just a random thought!

# Random Thoughts

- We all make mistakes and have lapses in judgment! It's by admitting our faults that we grow and mature! Just a random thought!

- Never underestimate the grace and power of God! All things are possible when you believe! Have faith! Just a random thought!

- If Christ can calm the raging seas, He can calm the raging seas of stress and anxiety in your life! Have faith and trust Him! Just a random thought!

# Random Thoughts

---

- When you speak God's Word, it's a deposit into your heavenly account! Just a random thought!

- Our righteousness *is not* of ourselves! But if you are in Christ, your righteousness is by the power of God! Just a random thought!

- It's said to choose your battles wisely! But what do you do if the battle chooses you? Is it fight or flight? Just a random thought!

- The devil says you're worthless! God says you're worthy! The devil says you can't! God says with Him you can! Just a random thought!

# Random Thoughts

---

- In God's hands, there are many opportunities! Are you in God's hands? Just a random thought!

- If you are in Christ, your anointing is greater than the evil around you! Just a random thought!

- Doing a little to improve your health is far better than doing nothing and getting a whole lot of nothing in return! Just a random thought!

- Don't spend your whole life trying to live that life! Someone needs to hear this! Just a random thought!

# Random Thoughts

- If God in Christ is first in your life, God in Christ is the centerpiece of your life! Just a random thought!

- You find contentment in all things when you are content in your relationship with God! Just a random thought!

- If you have a good idea but don't put it into practice, it's just a good idea! Just a random thought!

- Show and demonstrate as much love as you can! And then love some more! Just a random thought!

# Random Thoughts

- You grow in God when you allow God to grow in you! Are you growing? Just a random thought!

- Common sense is free! Oddly, some people live like they can't afford it! Just a random thought!

- The devil can't take what God has given you unless you choose to give it away! Just a random thought!

- Some can see but are blind to the truth! Others blind themselves to falsehoods so they can see the truth! Just a random thought!

# Random Thoughts

———◇◇◇◇◇◇———

- Don't speak about anything you don't know anything about as if you do know! Be silent until you know! Just a random thought!

- Be in the habit of making the right decisions! Wrong decisions result in wrong results! Just a random thought!

- If you need to change but don't want to change, you will never change! If you need to learn but don't want to learn, you will never learn! Just a random thought!

# Random Thoughts

- Don't complain about what's *on* the table if you didn't bring anything *to* the table! Just a random thought!

- It's by knowledge that we gain understanding! It is by understanding that our knowledge is increased! One enhances the other! Just a random thought!

- Don't complain about what's *on* the table if you didn't bring anything *to* the table! Just a random thought!

# Random Thoughts

—◆◆◆◆—

- As you grow, let your compassion for others grow as well! Just a random thought!

- God knows every detail of your life! God has detailed Himself in and through His Word! Just a random thought!

- You can't fight fire with fire if you don't have any fire burning within you! Just a random thought!

- The more seeds you plant, the more plants you'll grow! The more you learn of God, the more you'll know! Just a random thought!

# Random Thoughts

- To do something, you must know something about that something to do something! Just a random thought!

- How well do you know God? Well, God knows you better than you know yourself! Just a random thought!

- God's answer to those who thirst and hunger after righteousness is *Him*! Just a random thought!

- Nothing can be done unless you take the time to do it! You cannot know God unless you take the time to know Him! Just a random thought!

# Random Thoughts

- Does the person you present outwardly reflect the person you are inwardly? Just a random thought!

- Prayer must begin with preparation in your heart and mind to pray! Just a random thought!

- It's wise to make a habit of having good habits! Just a random thought!

- There are so many steps in life! Don't waste any of your steps walking the wrong path! Just a random thought!

# Random Thoughts

---

- Living a carefree life does not mean to live a careless life! Be careful in your care for yourself! Just a random thought!

- It's not our problems that move God! It's our faith in God to solve our problems that move God! Just a random thought!

- Without trust, there can be no faith! Without faith, there can be no hope! One enhances and embraces the other! Just a random thought!

# Random Thoughts

---

- A lack of faith and negative thinking can cancel the plans God has for you! But if you are strong in the spirit of faith, God's plans will come to pass! Just a random thought!

- Putting God first is not when you're just in need, but it's an everyday lifestyle that empowers you in the power of God! Just a random thought!

- Encouragement builds courage! Courage increases faith! Faith secures trust! Trust opens the doors of hope! Just a random thought!

# Random Thoughts

- We are to hold on to the good and rebuke the evil! But if you're weak in faith, you may be rebuked by what you want to rebuke! Just a random thought!

- You cannot fuel your faith without believing, and you cannot fuel your belief without faith! Just a random thought!

- Live to learn, and in your learning, learn to live! Just a random thought!

- Never take your frustrations at the workplace home! It's like working overtime and *not* getting paid! Just a random thought!

# Random Thoughts

- Praise to praise are the bookends to faith, hope, and trust in God! Just a random thought!

- Never allow anyone to use your past to ruin your future! Keep pressing forward in the plan God has for you! Just a random thought!

- Many cannot hear the voice of God because they are to consumed with listening to themselves! Just a random thought!

- There is no direction without knowledge and knowledge is useless without direction! Just a random thought!

# Random Thoughts

- Be watchful of the things you say and do! Remember, a scrambled egg cannot be unscrambled! Just a random thought!

- Hope without faith is hopeless! Having faith in your hope is a must! Just a random thought!

- Don't make misery your campground! Keep moving forward! Better days are ahead! Just a random thought!

- If you can't make time for someone, don't be offended if they don't make time for you! Remember, one hand washes the other! Just a random thought!

# Random Thoughts

- Be so strong in *faith* that your doubts doubt themselves! Let that sink in! Just a random thought!

- A lie that is sprinkled with the truth is *still* a lie! Just a random thought!

- God is willing to accept all! But those who go to heaven are those who accept God! Just a random thought!

- Every journey has a starting point! If you don't start, you'll never finish but slowly fade further away! Just a random thought!

# Random Thoughts

---◇◇◇◇◇---

- For many today, their inward impressions have become their outward expressions—hate, racism, bigotry, etc. How about expressing more *love*! Just a random thought!

- Often we see in others what we *want* to see and not what we *need* to see! Know the difference! Just a random thought!

- What you feed your mind becomes embedded in your heart! Out of the heart shows who you truly are! Be careful what you feed your mind! Just a random thought!

# Random Thoughts

- Using obscene and strong language doesn't make you any stronger, but it does expose your weak character! Just a random thought!

- You cannot reach your goal if you don't have a goal! Nothing plus nothing will always equal nothing! Just a random thought!

- We all have reasons to be proud of our children! Give your children reasons to be proud of you! Just a random thought!

- Are you impacted and influenced by others, or are they impacted and influenced by you? Just a random thought!

# Random Thoughts

- God's Word does not change! Nor should it be changed or rearranged! God has said what He has said! Just a random thought!

- I know I'm not perfect, but I strive for perfection! Why? Because I serve a perfect God! Just a random thought!

- A good teacher is open to more teaching! A good coach should also be coachable! A good preacher at times needs to be preached too! Always be open to growth! Just a random thought!

# Random Thoughts

- Your sin isn't justified by pointing out the sin of someone else! Sin is sin! Just a random thought!

- Someone is not a liar because they lie! They lie because they're a liar! Just a random thought!

- It's better to do something slowly with diligence and get it right than to rush right through it and get it wrong! Just a random thought!

- Apart from God, your struggles of today will feel like heaven compared to the hell that awaits you! Think about it! Just a random thought!

# Random Thoughts

- *Be proud but not prideful!* Just a random thought!

- It's not who you were but who you've become! Who you've become is who you are! Just a random thought!

- Have you received a word from God today? Better yet has God received a word from you? Just a random thought!

- You stand tallest on your knees when you kneel before God! Just a random thought!

# Random Thoughts

- What you learn today prepares you for tomorrow! What you learn tomorrow cannot help you today! Prepare today! Just a random thought!

- To experience the miraculous miracles of God, you must believe and experience God! Just a random thought!

- The here and now becomes the then and was! Make each day memorable! Just a random thought!

# Random Thoughts

- As we get older, we realize there are more days behind us than there are ahead of us! Cherish each day! Just a random thought!

- We do things to add years to our life! What are *you* doing to add life to your years? Just a random thought!

- I'd rather serve and be used by God than to serve and *be misused* by the world! Just a random thought!

- To be at peace, you must remain at peace with those who *are not* at peace with you! Just a random thought!

# Random Thoughts

—◈◈◈◈◈◈◈—

- The deeper you go into God, the higher your understanding becomes of God! Just a random thought!

- When you involve God in every area of your life, every area of your life is touched by God! Just a random thought!

- If you know of Christ and believe in Christ but *are not* living your life in Christ, you *cannot* grow in Christ! Just a random thought!

- Your life in this moment of time will determine your eternal life to come! Just a random thought!

# Random Thoughts

---

- Regardless of the day, when you stand and live your life in the presence of God, it's a good day! Just a random thought!

- If you give little or no time to God, don't feel bad if God does the same to you! You reap what you sow! Just a random thought!

- When in church, you are blessed by others, so out of church, you can bless others! Just a random thought!

- Many don't read the Bible because they say they don't understand it! Well, if you don't read it, you will never understand it! Just a random thought!

# Random Thoughts

- God cannot call on you to speak His Word if you don't know His Word! Just a random thought!

- Every day is a gift! What can you take from today you can use tomorrow and the tomorrows to come? Just a random thought!

# about the author

———◇◈◇◈◇———

The author Larry Dean Hill has been a constant student of the Bible since the late 1980s. Having read *every word* of the Bible over sixty times, Mr. Hill has spent thousands of countless hours over the years in researching the complete Bible from cover to cover. He endeavors to understand the customs and beliefs and the culture during Biblical times to fully grasp the scriptures in their entirety. He has dedicated his life to continue to faithfully spread the Word of God!